Surviving Anzio

Living in Nazi Italy
1943 and Beyond

Surviving Anzio

Living in Nazi Italy
1943 and Beyond

Sonia Di Tommaso Cucinotta

MERRIAM PRESS
WORLD WAR II MEMOIR 2
BENNINGTON, VERMONT
2015

First published by the Merriam Press in 2015

First Edition

ISBN 9781576384145
Library of Congress Control Number: 2015916408
Merriam Press #PC3-P

This work was designed, produced, and published in
the United States of America by the

Merriam Press
133 Elm Street Suite 3R
Bennington VT 05201

E-mail: ray@merriam-press.com
Web site: merriam-press.com

The Merriam Press publishes new manuscripts on historical subjects, especially military history and with an emphasis on World War II, as well as reprinting previously published works, including reports, documents, manuals, articles and other materials on historical topics.

Contents

Then

Now

Introduction

MY name is Sonia Di Tommaso Cucinotta. I am a naturalized American citizen. I came from Italy to the United States in 1955 with my 5 year-old son, Ambrose, where I was reunited with my beloved husband Marco Cucinotta in New York City. We made our home in Brooklyn and lived there until we retired to Florida. Recently, we have relocated to Maryland to be close to Ambrose.

Marco and I have been married for 66 years. Our son Ambrose has three children, Steven, Allison and Jon Michael.

I am now 87 years old. I have decided to write the history of my family's experiences during World War II. Much of what I experienced has not been described from the perspective of actually living in Italy during the Occupation of Anzio.

During that horrible time, my family home was seized and occupied by the Germans. My mother, father and I were allowed to stay in the same house in a small part of the kitchen. All of our other relatives — my brothers and sister — were forced to flee into hiding.

If I close my eyes, I can easily travel back to those frightening days. I can still hear the sounds of the cannons and feel how the vibrations rocked the house that we lived in. I can still smell the cordite from the explosions.

Many times, my life was in peril. I recognize that it was a miracle that I survived. I am certain God protected me many times from the hand of death.

With these thoughts in mind, I would like to dedicate this book to the Allied soldiers of World War II and to the Italian partisans. These men and women bravely fought the oppression and restored our liberty.

I pray to our Lord for all who fought for that cause and lost their lives. I pray too for their families suffering the loss of their loved ones, losses that last forever.

Through the sacrifices of so many, my beloved Marco, our wonderful son Ambrose and I were able to come to American and live our American dream. It is then with gratitude and reverence that I now begin my story.

For Marco

MARCO Cucinotta has been my husband for sixty-six years. I first met him when he was a young man and I was a fifteen year-old teenager. He came from Mili St. Marco which is in Messina, Italy.

Marco left Messina in August 1939. He attended the police academy in Castro Pretorio in Rome. After one month of training, he was given a horse and was told that he would be trained as a Carabiniere in the mounted police division. In August 1940, he was transferred to the Maccarese Province of Rome. In May 1941, he was transferred again, this time to Pomezia which is eighteen miles from Rome. There was a new police station in Pomezia, with a Commandant, or Maresciallo, and seven carabiniere and their horses.

Marco stayed in Pomezia until September 8, 1941. That day, a German soldier confronted him with a drawn pistol and demanded that Marco surrender his weapon.

"Italy is finished," said the soldier.

Thinking quickly, Marco gave up his weapon.

"Wait!" Marco said. "I will go and get the Commandant."

He entered the next room, closed the door and told everyone to escape out the back door thereby saving all of their lives.

He went to hide in a house where he knew the family which was not far from where we lived. After a short time, he came to help my father with some carpentry work. He stayed with us and became our adopted brother in order to escape the Germans. Marco was working underground with officers (generals for the Allied Forces) but never told us anything. We knew he was meeting officers but we knew nothing else. Even today, if I ask him about it, he will answer, "It's in the past, a long time ago."

War brought Marco into the life of my family. He became a son to my father, a protector to our family and a friend to me. When the war ended, Marco returned and asked me to marry him. It took me several days to decide to become his wife. When I was of an age to marry, Marco and I committed our lives to each other.

My affection for him began as a love for a brother transformed into a love of a woman for a man. He became the love of my life. After all of our years together, we are still in love.

Marco is almost ninety-four years old. His mind remains sharp and he is able to walk and also ride his bicycle.

We live in an apartment now in a home for the elderly. We have activities which include dancing. We are always ready for dancing.

I thank our Lord that we are still together. We pray that someday, when it is time for us to go to heaven that the Lord, in his Mercy, takes us home together.

When we returned to Pomezia in 2010, Signor Major Rodrigo Micucci was the head of the Police station and had given us an invitation for Marco and I to visit the station as it stands today. Corporal (Designee) Vincenzo Falisi, was at the police station that day and gave us a tour of where Marco was stationed before the German invaded Pomezia. Marco explained that much has changed. When the Signor Micucci asked Marco how it was that he was able to stay alive, we told him our story. It was so emotional that tears were streaming down from our eyes. He also urged me to write this story, this history should be known, Micucci said. We thanked Signor Falisi and Micucci, from the bottom of our heart for the hospitality they had shown us.

This book is for Marco, the love of my life.

Loreto Di Tommaso
My Father

WHEN my father was very young, he lost his mother and one sister in an earthquake. He never had a chance to go to school. His father was raising the children by himself until he met his second wife. She was never fond of his children.

The family had a large farm and everybody worked. He was a hard worker and everybody loved him. Once someone would meet him, they wouldn't know that he had never gone to school. Perhaps marrying my mother and listening to her perfect Italian, he learned many things.

As a farmer, he had constructed a wooden device to sow seeds in the ground, six rows at a time. He wanted to patent it but in those days money was in short supply. He had to give up the idea. In later years, I saw a similar machine made out of steel.

When my father met Marco for the first time, he told my mother that he thought Marco was a nice young man and a very hard worker. Little did he know that later, Marco would ask him and my mother for permission to marry me. They were very happy, because they loved him as a son. He lived at our house until the Allied Forces liberated Rome.

Angelina Pierri Di Tommaso
My Mother

SHE grew up in a convent after her father passed away at a very young age. She was of medium height, with green eyes and black hair and had very pleasant personality. She loved to sing and had a beautiful voice. She knew most of the famous Italian operas, and would recite the stories to us while we were growing up.

When my mother married my father, she had never cooked. My father told her, don't worry I'll teach you, and he did. She became a very good cook, so good, that her friends would ask her to cook for their daughters weddings. My mother also taught my sister and me to cook too. Her hands were always busy with sewing, embroidering, knitting and crocheting. She would make our clothes, even our sweaters and socks too. To prepare for the winter, she would can vegetables and preserves for the family.

Maria Di Tommaso Blancodini
My Sister

MY sister, Maria, lives in Pomezia, Italy. She is over 90 years old and her husband, Dario Blancodini died several years ago. It broke her heart

Vincenzo Di Tommaso
My Brother

MY brother, Vincenzo, was working with my father for a while. He then became a mechanic, repairing automobiles and trucks. He died from cancer at a young age.

Antonio Di Tommaso
My Brother

MY brother, Antonio, learned to become a tile setter and mechanic. He came to the United States after I filled his papers for immigration. It took a little longer because he was born in France. He came and stayed with us to live in Brooklyn, New York. After a while he got a job as an airframe mechanic with Pan American Airlines, he also had an interest in wedding photography on the weekends. Unfortunately, he also died a young age as well.

Cherchio, Abruzzo, Italy
1899

MY father, Loreto Di Tommaso was the third child born to Antonio Di Tommaso and his wife, Maria Malandra. Three other children would follow. The oldest child was a son, Gaetano, and a second son was Donato. My father Loreto and two daughters, Maria Carmina and Concetta, were born later.

When he was nine years old, there was big earthquake. My father and his brothers ran into the street and escaped the collapsing house. My grandmother and daughter Concetta were killed.

My grandfather and daughter Carmina survived by finding shelter in one corner of the house. They were imprisoned inside the destroyed structure for four days waiting to be rescued. God, in his mercy, sent rain to the area which permitted my grandfather and my aunt to have some water to drink. Without water, no one believed they would have survived.

As a widower, my grandfather raised the children and worked his farm. In 1915, World War I began. In 1916, my father was called into service. He was just seventeen years old.

He served in the Alpine Corps in Trento. In 1918, when my father returned from the war, he learned that my grandfather had met a woman named Carolina from a town called Abbadeggio in the Province of L'Aquila. Carolina consented to marriage and she joined Antonio on the farm.

All of the children were opposed to the marriage. The new stepmother treated the children badly. The brothers would return from working in the field with their father and Carolina would refuse to let the boys come in the house. They were forced to sleep wherever they could find a place to rest. She fed them lots of cooked potatoes as that was the crop my grandfather grew on his land.

Guagnano, Province of Lecce on the Adriatic Sea 1894

MY mother, Angela Pierri was born to Vincenzo and Adelaide Pierri. They earned their living through their own business. Unfortunately, my grandfather became ill. In an effort to care for her husband, my grandmother had to use whatever resources the family had. Soon those resources were exhausted. When my mother was eight years old, and her older brother Emilio was ten, her father died.

To deal with the difficulties of her life, Adelaide decided to place my mother in a convent with the nuns. My mother would provide work for the nuns who would in turn see to her education and room and board. Adelaide chose to keep Emilio with her. He stayed with his mother until he was 18 and enlisted in the Royal Police. Emilio became a sergeant and was sent to Abruzzo.

Once my mother became a young lady, she wanted to leave the convent. She studied to be a schoolteacher. The nuns taught her to do fine handwork. She learned also how to knit, crochet, and to sew. My mother also loved opera. She had a fine singing voice. She was of medium height, with green eyes and black hair. She also had a very pleasant personality.

Abruzzo
1920

FTER a few years in Abruzzo, Emilio married a woman named Concetta. My memory fails and I do not recall her last name. Emilio wrote to his mother and also to his sister, telling them both to come and live with him in Abruzzo. The two women left their home and moved in with Emilio and his new wife.

Predictably, Emilio's wife did not welcome her husband's mother and sister into her home. She wanted her husband all to herself. Family lore has it that she mistreated both women.

One day, my mother went to do some errands. She saw a handsome young man, Loreto Di Tommaso. According to my mother, they looked into each other's eyes and love blossomed at first sight. They talked to each other about their families and compared their problems with step relatives. My father's step-mother wanted him to marry her own granddaughter, an idea that repulsed him.

I have no idea, given the customs of the day, how these two young people found ways to meet and talk, but love will always find a way if it was meant to be. Three months after their first meeting, the two decided to marry. Somehow, the two were married, found a place to live and brought my grandmother, Adelaide, to live with them.

After the couple were married and settled in their own home, Concetta became ill and died. She and Emilio had no children. Emilio remained a widower for several years. Eventually he met Lucia Blancodini from Castelvecchio Subequo (AQ), which is also in the Province of Abruzzo. They fell in love and Lucia became Emilio's second wife. They had two children, a daughter Linda and a son, Enzo.

My parents, along with Grandmother Adelaide, settled into their home. Sadly, Adelaide died within a year of the marriage. She never had a chance to see any of her grandchildren except for my sister Maria.

The babies soon began to arrive in the Di Tomasso family. In 1922, my sister, Maria was born. Vincenzo followed in 1925. I arrived in 1928. My youngest brother, Antonio, was born in 1932 when our family was living in France.

As the oldest child, Maria had more status in the family than I did. I confess I always felt inferior to her. I did not have this feeling with Vincenzo because the chores he had to do were different from those given to my sister and me since he was a boy.

It always seemed to me that I always got worse chores to do than those given to Maria. I was almost a grown up when I realized this really wasn't the case. I was blessed with an inventive personality and I always tried to do something new with whatever was asked of me. I remember my mother speaking to me about this.

"Sonia," she said, you are always asking questions, looking at things, trying to figure out how they are done. "You are faster than your eyes!"

I think there was a lot of truth in what my mother said. Whenever my mother made me a dress or some other piece of clothing, I always wanted it to look different. Even if she gave me a pair of white socks, I would add color or some embroidered design to enhance the simplicity of the item.

I now believe that my parents selected chores for me to utilize my creativity in getting things done. I was never a timid child and was willing to attempt any challenge set before me. This quality set me apart from my sister and also my brother. It also explains why I, instead of any of my siblings, was asked to take so many more risks during the war. I believe my parents had confidence in me that if any of their children could survive the perils of war, it was likely to be me.

My sister Maria is now 91. Her family's home is in Pomezia, Italy. She and her husband, Dario Blancodini, had four sons. Dario died six years ago. They had been married for 66 years. My sister's heart was broken when she lost her beloved husband. She is blessed to live close to her sons and her grandchildren. She and I have often visited over the years and I love her very much.

My brother Vincenzo worked with my father for a number of years after the war then found a career as an auto mechanic. Sadly, cancer took him from us when he was a still young man.

My brother Antonio learned to set tile and also became an auto mechanic. He came to the United States after waiting six months from the time I filed his entry papers. The delay was due to having to get the additional clearance since he was born in France. While he lived with us in our house in Brooklyn, NY, Antonio worked for Pan American Airlines as an air frame mechanic. He also liked to do photography on the weekends. Unfortunately he died at a young age from cancer.

But I am getting ahead of myself. As my parents dealt with their growing family, the times they were living in grew increasingly difficult. Jobs became scarce. In 1929, my mother and father determined that the only way to support the family would be for my father had to go to Belgium and work in the mines.

Being a miner is not easy work. It was especially difficult for my father because his lungs had been injured during World War I from inhaling toxic gasses. Breathing in the mines was difficult for him.

He decided to move to Cognac, France where he thought he could find better work. He did find a job there and a place for all of us to live, but soon after, we moved to Salegnes.

Cognac, France
1931

WE traveled to France to be with our father. We were all very happy there and a year after we arrived, Antoine was born in 1932.

Our life as a family became routine. My mother taught Maria and I, everything she knew about home making. Her hands were always busy. She taught us to cook and to sew, to knit and crochet, to do embroidery and fine hand work. She made our clothes, knitted our socks and our sweaters.

To prepare for winter, she would can vegetables and make preserves for the family. Her cooking became so good; her friends would often ask her to cook for the weddings of their children.

War began to creep across Europe. In June 1938, my parents began quarrelling. Their arguments grew stronger and more frequent. I did not understand what was going on. I was just a child of 10. But it soon became clear: my father wanted our family to move back to Italy and my mother did not want to go.

Wives didn't oppose their husbands very much back then. My father stated we were definitely going back. My mother, angry and resistant, told him no!

I remember my mother, screaming back at my father, "We are not going!!"

My father became very angry. "Yes, we are going back," he responded loudly.

All four of us children started to cry. I don't remember which of us spoke up, but somebody said, "We will stay in France with Mamma!!"

My father shook his head, weary of the arguing.

"You do not understand," he said to all of us. "They are talking about a war and I am not going to fight against my brothers!"

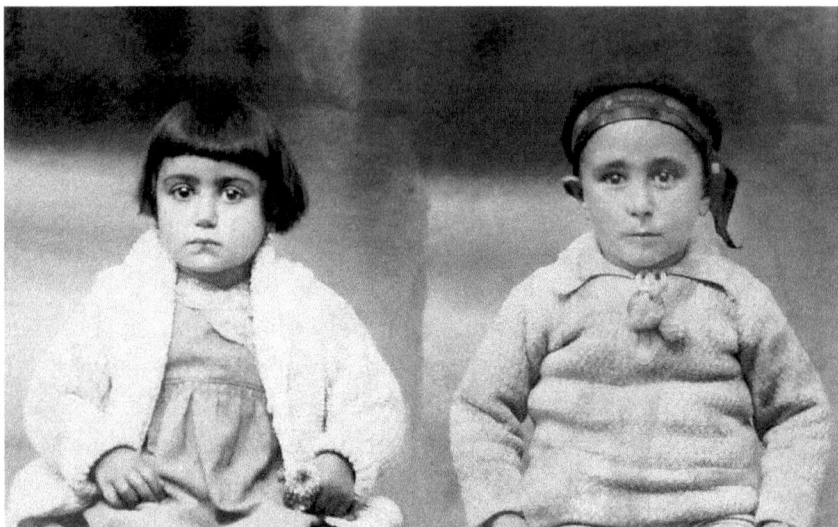

Sonia and brother Vincenzo just arriving in France

For days, the arguments continued, growing worse and worse. Harsh words and tears filled our house. The people of the town found out about the discord in the house. Some came to my mother and told her to let my father go, that he had a head like Mussolini. They told her if she stayed, they would help her, and that she would be okay.

My mother was a realist. She realized she couldn't stay in France with four children without her husband. Loreto was determined to return to his homeland. She decided she had no choice and the decision was made. We were all going back to Italy.

My parents went to the Italian embassy. When they came home, my parents said that according to the embassy, Mussolini was reaching out to all Italians outside of Italy. Mussolini promised any Italians responding to his call to return to Italy would receive compensation in Italy for what they left behind in other countries. "I assure you," he was quoted to my parents by the embassy, "We will give back whatever you lost."

I believe this made it easier for my mother to accept our return. Before many more days passed, the consulate in France

Di Tommaso Children
Left to right: Vincenzo, Maria, Antonio, Sonia

Maria and me, front center, with friends in France

gave my parents the papers they needed to go back Italy. We packed up all we could and traveled by train in June 1939 with all us of crying the entire way.

Di Tomasso family with friends in Salegnes, France

I recall just a few of the names of the places we traveled through on our journey back to Italy. We stopped at some hotels going along the coast—Costa Azzurra. The mountains were covered with geraniums. I was eleven years old when we made that trip. But even today, so many years later, if I close my eyes I can still see those mountains awash in the red flowers. This was just before we crossed the border into Italy. I remember seeing a sign for Bardonecchia and Ventimiglia.

Avezzano, Italy
1939

IT took us eight days to arrive at Avezzano where my Uncle Emilo and his wife, and our Aunt Lucia lived with their two children, Linda and Enzo. The house was small and they were renters. Getting us all to fit in their home was difficult.

There just was not much room for all us in our Uncle Emilio's home. My cousin Linda slept in her parent's room. My sister and I slept in the room with my mother and father. The boys slept in another room altogether. Everything was very tight.

During the day we played in front of the house. We had a jump rope. We played with pebbles in a game we invented. We would put four pebbles on the ground, take another pebble, toss it in the air and try to pick up all four pebbles on the ground before we caught the pebble we'd thrown in the air. If you missed, you had to give up a pebble. We also played cards.

Fortunately, the weather was not to hot and stayed pleasant until the fall when it started to get cold.

Three of us, Vincenzo, Antoine and myself, went to school in Avezzano for one year

My mother soon realized we had to find a place of our own.

Almost every day, my mother would go to the government offices to try and get for us what the Italian embassy said Mussolini had promised. She wanted the government to take care of us, to find us an apartment. But the government was not doing anything to help us. My mother went from one office to another, yelling, "I have four children to feed!! We cannot stay with my brother any longer."

One day, a government official spoke to her and threatened her. He said, "Signora Di Tommaso, if you keep coming every day, one of these days you are going to be arrested. You cannot continue to act like this."

*Maria and Sonia for a reunion with childhood friends
in Salegnes, France*

Maria and Sonia with French friends

Cousin Linda shared her family's house after leaving France

My mother responded, "If you arrest me, are you going to take care of my four children?"

Why, you might ask, did my mother go to plead our case instead of our father? My mother was brave and she wise. She said to my father so that all of us could hear, "If you go to the government offices, they will arrest you. I am a woman with children to care for. They can't do anything to me." She truly believed this. She continued to go to the offices demanding help.

After what seemed a long time, I think it was almost November, the government found us an apartment for which the government would pay the rent. It was in Avezzano on Vittorio Emanuel II. I think it was #10. We moved in to the apartment in November 1939.

Linda's brother, cousin Enzo

One of the conditions for us to get the apartment from the government required my mother to register all of us children in school and to promise that all of us would become members of the Fascist party. My mother, always the negotiator, told the government that she would sign us up for school but she would not permit her children to join the Fascist party.

This made the official furious. Yelling at my mother, he said, "You will do what we say or there will be severe consequences!"

My mother backed down. She was afraid that maybe the government would separate us. With no alternative, she had to do what she was told. We were registered in school and became members of the Fascist party.

Our first year in Italy was difficult for the Di Tommaso family but we made it through. All around us the war was intensifying. Young Italian men were being called to arms. My father received the call to the army early in 1940. He was 41 years old and had already fought in World War I.

He told the army recruiter, "I am too old to be in the army. "

The recruiter responded by saying, "Don't worry, you are not too old to take care of the horses."

My mother was not going to take her husband's being drafted sitting down. She went from one office to another seeking help. Her efforts paid off. One day she was told by an official that the following week the entire family was going to be sent to Italian Barce in Libya by boat. The boat would leave from Civitavecchia and there the family would receive additional information.

My mother answered, crying, "You called my husband into the army even though he is old and all we have. We are not going without my husband. What would we do without him for something to live on? What are we going to do?"

The official, most likely worn down by my mother's persistence, responded, "Don't cry — we will take him out of the army." Once again, my mother had succeeded in saving our family. Perhaps the official had also succeeded at removing a thorn in his side and was most likely looking forward to my mother and our family leaving.

A month went by before my father came back home. By that time, of course we had long missed the boat we were supposed to take. We later learned that the boat to Tripoli had sunk and everyone aboard had perished.

Our family was struggling financially. We had used up all the money we had brought with us from France. My father found some odd jobs to work whenever he could. My sister Maria and my mother did hand work for customers who wanted crocheted collars and the like. None of the work was sufficient to feed us. With winter coming, we would need to find some way to heat the apartment, as Abruzzo winters were cold and harsh. When the snow would come, we would not even be able to open the door.

My mother became friends with Signora Annita Nurzia. She and her husband, Felice Nurzia were in the business of transporting coal on the railroad. Signora Annita told my mother to send the children when the coal arrived to the railway station. That way, we could pick up whatever fell to the ground and that might be some help to warm the family up.

"I will let you know what day and the time the train will pull into the station," Signora Annita said.

"God bless you, Annita!, my mother responded, grateful for the prospect of help for us.

Signora Annita was true to her word and told my mother when the train would arrive. That day, when Vincenzo, Antoine and I came home from school, our mother met us at the door.

"Hurry, hurry!" My mother yelled, "It's almost time for the train."

I ran with my brothers to the train station. Back in those days, the coal came in burlap sacks that closed at the top. Wooden sticks were used to secure the tops of the bags and when the coal workers opened the bags, the sticks were thrown to the ground. We hurriedly picked up the sticks and made bundles of them to bring home. We would use them to warm up the kitchen and for Mamma to cook. Occasionally, some coal would fall to the ground and we had bags to put it in to bring home. Sometimes, the workers would make some coal fall off the train. They would smile at us as we picked up the coal. I remember we were all so very young. I think I was almost 13, which made Vincenzo 16 and Antoine 8.

After moving from France to Abruzzi, my sister, Maria, standing left, and I, had best friends Alfonza and Catarina Cornacchioli

Our lives were very difficult. I remember saying my prayers at bedtime one night. I was crying. I prayed to Saint Anthony to help us come out of the situations we were in. I prayed, "Saint Anthony, please help us. I promise I will donate a statue of you." Many years later when life was indeed much easier, I kept my promise to Saint Anthony. The statue was donated and is in the Church of Saint Benedetto in Pomezia, outside of Rome. For, in his own time, Saint Anthony answered my prayers and saved our family.

The year 1941 was especially difficult. Despite my mother's persistence with the government officials, no one would listen to her anymore or do anything to help her.

To help see us through the times with little food, my mother bought sacks of potatoes and put them in the basement of Signora Aurelia, our landlady. One day my mother told us to go get some potatoes to make supper. When we went to get the potatoes, we found them to be almost all gone. We came back and told mama that the potatoes were almost finished.

"That is not possible," she scolded us. "Come downstairs and see," we told her.

Mamma went to the basement with us. She could not believe what she found: The potatoes were indeed almost gone. Our landlady used to go to church every morning at the first mass. It was still dark at that time and she would use a candle to light her way. She would come down, candle in hand, and help herself to our potatoes. Mamma found where the candle wax had dripped on the potatoes so we knew for sure it was Signora Aurelia.

Mamma shook her head in disgust. How could our landlady steal from us when we were so poor and just surviving?

Mamma continued to go to the government officials pleading our case for help. Over and over she was told, "Signora, we need more time to find a way to help you—we have nothing to give your family at this time."

My mother and father knew something had to change. With little possibility for government support, my parents were forced to make a tough decision. Our father's brother, Gaetano Di Tommaso, operated a restaurant in Borgo Grappa which was near the city of Latina. Back then, the city was called Littoria. It was in the region of Agro Pontino. Mussolini had built that region up as he had the Agro Romano region. Originally the area was all swamp. Mussolini had directed the building of canals, dried out the swamp and made cities and towns in both regions — Agro Pontino and Agro Romano. When the land dried out, Mussolini divided the land, built homes for farmers, and hand-picked who would be selected to live in the regions. Some people were chosen because were the poorest or most in need. Some were chosen because they were recommended.

Longhorn cows, tilling soil on the farm
that Mussolini's Government promised us

My parents thought to ask Gaetano for help. Maybe he could find some answer for our desperate situation. Our uncle Gaetano was the oldest of my father's brothers. As the head of my father's family, Gaetano was determined to help our family. He contacted anyone he knew who might take pity on our situation. With Gaetano working on his side and my mother still pressing our case with local officials, the government finally assigned us a small farm in the Agro Romano region, about 25 miles from Rome. The farm had a house and some land. It was the smallest farm and the last one built in Pomezia. There was a brook, which separated this farm from the next property.

It was June when we were given our house. The weather was very mild and we walked from the train station to Le Tre Cannelle (Pomezia), our new home, a distance of about 6 or 7 kilometers. There really was no other way to get there.

We were happy to see our new home. The house had 3 bedrooms on the second floor and an additional room on the first floor near the large kitchen. There was no basement and no attic.

Years later when Marco was with us, he made an attic with an opening that you could not see—a hidden door. And, with some help, he fashioned a ladder out of rope. This was our secret hiding place. The men in our house would hide in this place when the Germans came.

Outside in the yard, there were two cows, and one horse.

My father worked to divert a portion of a brook to use on our crops so that he could grow all kinds of vegetables for our family and also sell for income. The brook was called the Rio Torto and it went down stream to Tre Cannelle which meant the three jets of water. There the water went into a big long fountain not very far from our farm. The fountain was built many years before to provide drinking water for the wild life in the area. On the other side, the brook went to the ocean near Ardea which is not too far from Anzio.

Life was getting a little better for us although there was lots of work to do for everyone. My job was to go to school every day in Pomezia. My little brother Antonio was also going to school. We had one bicycle between us. Because I was older, I was the one to pedal the bike with the two of us riding. When we came to a hill, we would walk. On the last hill before reaching the school, we passed the police station—Caserma Carabinieri. Often the carabinieri would look at us from the window. I could see them talking and I would say to myself—"You carabinieri are lucky—you have horses. You don't have to walk like us and have two of us on one bicycle."

Maria and Dario soon after they were engaged

One good thing—we never had to deal with snow in the winter. Pomezia is about 25 miles from Rome and the weather was not so cold.

My brothers, Antonio and Vincenzo in Pomezia in later years

My complaining didn't change the situation. Antonio and I continued to ride and walk to school. We started school where we all had to learn Italian. The school authorities put us two classes behind but in no time we caught up. In the Tre Cannelle, my brother Antonio and I earned our fifth grade diploma just in time as the war threatened. My mother helped us.

Later in life when I was in America, I promised myself that I would learn English. I went to night school at New Utrecht High School in Brooklyn, and at the same time, I was learning a trade and caring for our son Ambrose and my husband. When Marco would come home, he would help with Ambrose so that I could go to school and study. We were both very happy when I earned my language certificate.

In 1942, my sister, Maria was almost 18. Through my Aunt Lucia, my sister met Dario Blancodini. Dario had just finished school and had his teaching degree. Maria and Dario fell in love. I can tell you this—my parents were not happy.

"This is no time for a wedding," my parents told Maria and Dario. "What if we have to leave this area and go somewhere else?"

But love is love. Maria and Dario continued to see each other, telling our parents that they would wait for their wedding.

At this time, Dario was teaching in Abruzzo. He had a temporary assignment. He wanted to teach in Pomezia and had filed a request for transfer. He was still finishing up some of his studies at the University of Naples.

The army recruiter found Dario and Dario joined the army. On his right sleeve, the army insisted he wear a badge which showed a logo "VU"—which meant that he was Voluntary University. What this meant was that he had voluntarily joined the army. Dario used to laugh at this, saying he was forcefully called to join the army—there was not much of anything voluntary.

The army sent Dario to the city of Trani. This was in 1942. Maria and Dario wanted to get married. Dario put in a request for leave time to get married but his superiors declined his request. Dario wrote to Maria saying, if she were to come and beg his superiors, perhaps they would have pity and grant Dario leave.

When my sister told this to my mother and father, they became furious. "This is insane," my mother said. "We don't have all that money for us to send you and Sonia to Trani. We have made the preparations for a wedding here. The white gown is here. We are ready here—not in Trani."

Maria wouldn't listen. She loved Dario and she would make the trip to Trani alone.

All my mother could do was weep. "Maria, what can I tell you?" Alone, Maria went to Trani. Two days later, Maria and Dario returned together. They had traveled by train to Rome and then taken a bus from Rome to Pomezia. From there they had walked the three kilometers to Le Tre Cannelle.

My mother took Maria aside and confronted her with the white wedding gown.

"My dear daughter," my mother said, "if you can't wear this white gown, I will forgive you. You can wear something else!"

Maria started to cry. "Mamma, I'll wear the gown because in front of our Lord I am not afraid to wear it. I have not sinned."

The two were married in church on Sept. 27, 1942. A week later, Dario went back to his army post in Trani. My sister Maria stayed with us at Tre Cannelle. My sister and Dario were married for almost 65 years until Dario's death in 2005.

After the wedding, our house became even more crowded. We had two sisters from Rome, Dora and Daria. Dora taught at Santa Procula, a school not far from us. The two came to us because they were afraid to stay in Rome. Their brother, Dino, came from Rome to stay occasionally. Guiseppe Gentile and his wife Carmela and their four children — Ugo, Annetta, Mario and Titina stayed with us because their house was a potential target for bombing at the crossroad near Pomezia. We had another family that came from Rome; although I do not remember their names. I do remember that they had a little girl that was sick. I don't know what was wrong with her. They came to us because they feared the Americans bombing from Anzio. As I think back, I remember there was one other family, with two children, a boy and a girl. More than twenty people were in that house at Tre Cannelle.

Every so often, my brother in law Dario came on furlough to see Maria. Fortunately, his application to teach in Pomezia was accepted. This was especially good as my sister Maria was expecting their first child at the end of June 1943.

All this time, the war was intensifying. Some Italians joined with the Germans and called themselves the Republica Di Saló. The Italians that would not go with the Germans and Republica Di Saló were called Partigiani or Partisans. How sad this was — Italians killing Italians!

Food shortages in Rome prompted people to leave the city to search the surrounding areas for food. One of my father's friends was Colonel Racalbuto. One day he came to the farm to buy food. He had a very worried expression. My father and mother asked him what was wrong.

The colonel started to weep as he told the story of what had happened a few days earlier. The Germans wanted to arrest him to get military information. The Germans planned to arrest captains, lieutenants, and generals. They took them to the Via Tasso, in Roma. Via Tasso was a place of torture that the Germans used. When they arrested a suspicious person whom they suspected of working with the underground, the Germans would use torture to gain information. They would pull out fingernails; pour cement up to a person's neck until he died and other torture. Many died at Via Tasso.

The Germans knocked on his door and told him to come with them to be questioned. He told the Germans he had nothing to tell them as he was retired. As they were forming to leave with him, one of the German soldiers bumped the piano. When the piano hit the wall, it knocked down a picture of Hitler which hung on the wall. One of the Germans picked up the picture.

"What is this?" he asked the colonel.

The colonel responded, "The Fuhrer sent this to my daughter, Francesca Racalbuto as she painted a picture of him and sent it him. He sent her this photo to thank her."

Surprised, the Germans saluted the colonel and said to him— "You are a lucky man. This photo saved your life."

On another occasion, I went on an errand for my mother not too far from our home, when the sirens started to warn of an attack. Everyone was running as I entered the shelter. I saw a little girl in mother's lap, the father next to them. The mother was trying to protect the little girl from the cold because the shelter was underground and very cold. The little girl had only her panty and under shirt. I told the mother, the baby is cold. Why doesn't she have something warmer on, that the child was going to get sick dressed like that.

The mother, crying, replied, "We had to run for our lives. They bombed our house. We have nothing and nowhere to go." They had come from another town.

When the danger was over and the siren whistled to go home, I told them to come to my house. They were very happy when we got to the house. My mother and father told them they could stay for one week but then they would have to go home to see what had happened to their own place. While all the discussion was going on, I went to look what I could do for that poor little girl without a dress on her back. I was looking for some material and there was none. But I found an Italian flag, which was quite large. I decided to make a dress for her out of the flag. I made the top white, the skirt green, and the sleeves red. I sewed everything by hand. When I finished the dress and put it on the little girl, the mother and father started to cry. "My God, my God," the mother said, "Our little girl has a dress." She turned to my mother and said, "You have saved our lives. Thank you." Then she turned to me and she said, "God bless you for what you did for us today."

After a week, they left us. We never found out if they survived the war. On June 30, 1943, my sister Maria gave birth to a baby boy. She named him Berardino. We called him Dino. But my bother-in-law Dario, the baby's father, was still with the military in Trani. My sister cried. "I hope my baby will get to see his father," she said between her tears.

The Americans bombed Rome that year although I don't remember the date. They hit San Lorenzo. My brother Vincenzo was in the vicinity of the bombing. He came home shaken. "The

Americans bombed near Piranimide. Also near the hospital Regina Margherita," he said.

It was not long after this that a committee with the Pope made an agreement with the Allies not to destroy all the precious works of art. Then on August 14, 1943, they declared Roma and open city, Roma Citta Aperta.

Once Rome was declared an open city, the people that were in our house, left to go to Rome. They said, "Now, maybe we will be safer in Rome."

On September 8, 1943 General Eisenhower signed a treaty in Cassibile, Sicily with the Italian king, Umberto II Di Savoia. We were told that the king asked General Eisenhower to wait 24 hours to dispatch the treaty. This would give the King time for his army to ready themselves to go up against the Germans. The news of the signing of the treaty was dispatched immediately. The Germans occupied Italy and then defeated the Italian army. Battles broke out all over the city.

Our soldiers and the police force were stunned and did not know what do. The Germans took them all prisoners and then let them go. The Italian soldiers started to walk back to their hometown. They had no food and only the clothes on their back. When they passed our house, my mother used to give them a loaf of bread and whatever we else could give them. She would give them the food and say, "God be with you." We made bread all day and every day. We never found out if those poor soldiers made it to their homes and families.

Before the Armistice of September 8, 1943, the sergeant of the Police, Brigadiere Proietti, came to our house with a bundle inside a uniform and said to my father, "I need your help. In this bundle, I have all the papers from the police station. Please, see what you can do to save them. Someday we will have our Italy back and we will need these papers.

My father started to think. Where could he hide the papers that they would be safe? He pointed outside of our house, and he told the sergeant, "We will keep them safe." He had pointed to the oven outside in the yard. It was like a little house next to our house. It had a tile roof. My father quickly started to uncover the roof. He placed the papers in the roof, making sure that they were secure and then he replaced the tiles.

As the Brigadiere left, he told my father, "Thank you, Signor Di Tommaso." At the end of the war, when we went home, we thanked God that the oven house was still standing. My father removed the roof tiles and returned the papers to the police station.

The Maresciallo Tomassini, the officer at the police station, "This is something I never expected to see returned to the caserma, (the police station.) I have no words on how to thank the Di Tommaso family.

About a week after the armistice of Sept. 8, 1943, my brother-in-law Dario came home. He walked the entire way from the city where he was stationed. He also found good Italians wherever he passed who gave him food and sheltered him from the Germans. When he arrived at our house and saw his baby boy, he started to cry. "I never thought I would be able to get to Pomezia and see everyone and meet my baby Dino."

A week later, Dario took a carriage with horses and went to the school in Pomezia. He got as many benches as could from there and loaded them into the carriage and brought them to our house. He told everyone he met to contact as many people as they could and tell them that whoever had children and wanted to send them to school, he would begin to teach them. Following this effort, children came to school and the room in our house was full of students every day.

Two months later, my father was talking to my mother. He told her that he needed to build a big shed. "I need some help to build the shed, someone with experience."

My mother spoke up. "I was talking to my friend, Comin's wife, and she told me that there is a policeman (carabinieri) at their house since the armistice. The policeman worked as a carpenter. It was what he did before joining the police force. Maybe I can get him to help you."

The young man was from Sicily my mother explained. "He can't go home now because the Americans invaded Sicily. He

Marco Police Academy Grad

Marco in full uniform at police station

would never to make it back to Sicily with the Germans stopping everyone they see, taking them to trains and sending them to nobody knows where."

The next day my father went to Signore Comin's home and met the young man. His name was Marco Cucinotta. My father explained about the shed and asked Marco if he would come to help build it. Marco replied that he would help.

The next morning, Marco came to our house. He introduced himself to my mother. My mother asked him how he had escaped the Germans. Marco shook his head and started to tell us.

On the 8th of September, the (maresciallo) commander sent me to the police station at Santa Palomba to deliver some important papers. I rode my bicycle. As I returned to Pomezia and was approaching the police station, I saw Germans near the door. I got down from the bicycle and approached the door.

A German soldier near the door said to me, "Italy is kaput. Italy is caput! Give me your weapons."

I had my revolver ready to shoot. I looked behind him and saw another soldier with a machine gun, also ready to shoot. I thought to myself, if I kill this one, the machine gun would kill me and all of my colleagues and superiors. I surrendered my gun to him with the gun pointed at the German. I went inside where everybody had already been taken prisoner.

After 24 hours they released all of us. We all ran and that is when I asked Signore Comin if I could sleep under the hay stack. Signore Comin made a hole in the hay and I climbed in. He then covered it over to make sure the Germans would not see that I was inside. It worked for a while until some insects came. I had to get out and then I started to sleep in the fields."

My mother said, "You can stay here with us."

We later learned that Marco was from Mili San Marco, near where Messina's City Hall stands today. It is across from Calabria, the mainland of Italy.

Marco told us that his father, Ambrogio Cucinotta, was in America with his sister, Frances and his brother, Santo. His mother Vincenza was still in Mili San Marco with three of his sisters, one of whom was married and lived upstairs from his mother. He had another brother who was a carabiniere and was stationed in Calabria.

"I wonder what has happened to all of my family?" he said softly. My father and Marco began to work on the shed. When they had finished building the shed, Marco told my mother and father that he would return to his home in Sicily.

"Where will you go?" my mother said. "You can't go to Sicily. You'll get killed before you get there. You have to cross the Strait of Messina. You will never survive!"

"Marco," my father said, "You will stay with us. We have four children. From this day forward, we have five children. You stay with us. If we live, you live. If we die, you will die with us."

So it was that Marco became one of our family.

On January 21, 1944, my father said to me, "Sonia, tomorrow morning, you need to get up early. You will come with me. We are going to our friend's house near Torvaianica."

General Dwight D. Eisenhower at Cassibile, Sicily

Torvainica is near the beach. I did not ask for any explanation. The next morning, Jan. 22, I did as I was told. I got ready and we started walking. When we were about half way there, I commented to my father, "Look Papa, see how red the sky is and yet there is no wind."

My father chuckled, "Don't you see? The sun is starting to come up."

As he said that, there was a very loud noise—like an explosion! Everything seemed to be trembling and shaking. We stopped as more explosions came.

"Sonia!" my father yelled, "Let's run home! These are the sounds of canons. Run!"

My father knew what was happening. He had fought in the First World War from 1915 to 1918. He was 18 when he called to fight in Trento, north of Italy. He was in the Alpine Corps. He knew what canons sounded like.

When we got home, my mother thanked God we had made it.

Marco and Marco's brother, Antonino

Marco's brother, Antonino, at the Rome Royal Police Acadamy

We all wanted to know what was happening. That day was the longest day I have ever known. We could not move to find out what was happening. Finally a man from Nettuno near Anzio told us, the Americans had landed in Anzio!

We all thanked God but we still wondered what was going to happen next.

Brother-in-law, Marco, Marco and Antonino in Milli San Marco

My father and Marco wanted to find other work but the war was intensifying. We all wondered what we were going to do. There were a lot of people at our house and more were coming.

Giuseppina, Me, Marco, Mamma Cucinotta,
Antonino and Angelina

We were trying to think what to do. We all believed if the Americans were coming, the war will be over soon. Two days passed with the cannons shooting all the time. The second night about 8 P.M., it was very dark outside; we heard noises outside — big metal noises.

My mother and father told us all to be quiet. We had a carbide lantern. This was a light with some kind of stone. When water was dripped on the stone it made a gas and the gas made a flame that produced a bright light. We shut off the lantern and used a candle instead. Our windows had black material on them to prevent any light from showing through.

As everything was silent, we heard a knocking at the door and a loud voice saying," Camerati! Camerati! Open the door."

My father went to the door and a few German soldiers came in. They made us understand that they wanted the house for their purposes and they wanted it soon. Then they left.

Very early next morning we all got up. We all asked, what are we going to do?

Santo, Elda, Ambrose, and me, soon after we arrived
in America in 1955, at the Brooklyn Botanical Gardens

The German lieutenant returned and spoke to my parents. He primarily used sign language. He said that our family could have the one room down by the kitchen and that the Germans would share the kitchen with us. The Germans would occupy the upstairs bedrooms.

He pointed to my mother and father indicating that he wanted them to go downstairs. He pointed at my brother and me, and told us to go with the others.

I got up and said, I have to help my mother. After speaking sign language, the Lieutenant asked if we spoke any other language. Perhaps he had noticed my accent. My mother told him that we all spoke French.

"Wonderful," he said, "Now we will be able to understand each other as I also speak French."

My father went outside in the morning to see what was going on. He came back with his eyes wide open.

"There are two canons outside, the biggest cannons that there are. There are lots of ammunition and so many soldiers. Unbelievable that they are putting one cannon next to our house and I think the other will be next to our neighbor's house." Our neighbors were the Busti family.

All the men got together and agreed to make a shelter underground, near the brook. There was a big slope, which would make the structure easier to build. The water access would be a definite advantage.

Working non-stop in shifts, the men made a shelter for 45 people. The shelter was made seven yards long at the end of the tunnel. The men agreed to leave a tin wall and start another tunnel back to back. The second tunnel was more than seven yards with a separate exit. This way if the tunnel were blown up in the bombing, there would still be a way to escape. Ventilation pipes for air were added. The men built benches along the sides, sort of like bunk beds. They put straw on the floor for the children. The grown up got the benches. My brother Antonio complained all the time. His place was on a piece of floor that slanted and he could never sleep. But, as it turned out, he was assigned that spot because it was close to the exit since he needed to use the toilet often. It seemed, every time he heard the sound of the cannons he had to go to the bathroom because he was so afraid.

Marco's sister Frances, husband Joe on left and their children on right and my son Ambrose in the middle

We got busy. Everybody that was in our house went to the excavated shelter, except for Mamma, Papa and me.

The lieutenant talked to us and said, 'When we are going to shoot the canon, we will knock at your door first to let you know. When you hear the sound, open your mouths. If you do not, you will burst your ear drums."

For a few days, the soldiers knocked, but after that we were on our own. When the cannons fired, the house trembled. The American troops also were firing back and when we heard the cannons, we just prayed that God would help us. A minute after the shooting when we heard the whistling, we thanked God that the bomb hadn't hit our house. The bomb did not hit our house while we were there.

Our kitchen was big and the soldiers set up a very big looking tank, which was like a pressure cooker. They cooked lots of potatoes and other food.

My mother and father started to cook for everybody in the shelter. When we counted everybody, there were 45 people. Every family took what they had from their house. The women

Left, Marco's brother-in-law Joe, sister, Frances, me, and in-laws, Elda and Marco's brother Santo. Ambrose blowing out candles

went into the fields and picked as many vegetables as they could find. I went with a bucket with the food my father cooked. When there was shooting, I would throw myself on the ground. When the shooting stopped, I would run as fast as I could. Everybody used to tell me to be careful, to stay with mama and papa.

But I answered them. "You have to eat." I was the only one the lieutenant would allow to go back and forth.

The days passed by and the battles were getting worse, especially at night. We could hear the sound of the tanks. The sky looked as though fireworks were everywhere.

Among the German soldiers there was a young man named Peter. He was from Poland. He had been stationed in Abruzzo and had learned some Italian before he came to our house.

Each night before the soldiers went back to the battlefield, they would say, "Tonight we send the American back into the ocean." When they came back, Peter would tell us, it is not the truth—the Americans are strong."

Marco's brother, Santo, and his three sisters,
finally reunited after a lifetime of separation

During the day, I was very busy. Besides going back and forth helping my mother and father with food, I had to wash clothes for the family, especially for my sister Maria's baby. He was only a few months old.

I did all the wash by hand. We had a tub outside and we pumped the water from the well. One day the soldier who attended the lieutenant, came to me and with sign language, told me to wash the clothes that he had in his hand. I made the sign, "No! No! No!"

Finally, I gave in thinking that I will do it this time but I will not do it anymore. And that was what I told him.

A few days later he came to me again. And I made the sign "No! No! No!" He picked up his arm and came close to me and touched my face, caressing my right cheek. I raised my hand and with all the strength

I had, I slapped him in the face. You could see the red of five fingers on his face. I was stunned. All the soldiers that were outside started saying something in German, something that I could not understand. I heard the lieutenant talk to the soldiers in German from the window. I kept hearing them say "Sonia, Sonia."

At that moment, I said to myself that they are going to shoot me, and maybe all of us. But I was also thinking what else they might do to me.

The lieutenant came quickly down the stairs. He asked every soldier what happened. Then he came over to me and speaking in French, he asked me what had happened. I told him the soldier wanted me to wash his clothes and also the lieutenant's clothes. I did it once and I told him not to come back again. That it was his job to do the laundry. He came to me and he touched my face.

"Nobody may touch my face," I said angrily. "Nobody may touch my face."

He looked at me and he told me I was right, that the soldier should never have touched my face.

After all that, he spoke to the solder and went with him inside. I heard the lieutenant talking to the soldier very loudly. Thankfully, that was the end of it.

The weeks went by. Airplanes flew low; the sound of machine gunfire was getting worse. I continued to deliver the food and wash the clothes, despite the guns and the bombs. I think I must have come to believe I was never going to get hurt, that I was somehow invincible.

One day I told my sister Maria that the baby needed a bath. She had been cleaning the baby with a washcloth. I told her to give him to me and I will give him a quick bath and bring him back to her. She said no. She asked if I was crazy. I tried to convince her and said that today, everything was calm. No sounds of guns. Finally she said that I could take the baby. I wrapped Dino in a blanket and started to go as fast as I could.

As I was almost halfway to the house, an airplane with machine guns started to shoot very low. I threw the baby on the ground and then myself on top of the baby. I cried to God to save my sister's baby. "O God, take me — save the baby, please save Dino."

The shooting ceased. I got up in a great hurry, and ran back to the shelter. My sister Maria was screaming — "My baby! My baby! I told Sonia I didn't want her to take Dino. I was afraid."

When everybody saw the baby and me alive—well there are no words to describe it. I never asked her again, and I thanked God for saving baby Dino and me. I know it was God's help because the shrapnel and the bullets were very close to the two of us.

Days went by. Again, one day while washing clothes, I heard an airplane overhead. The Germans started to shoot around the house as the airplane came even closer. I saw it was a German airplane they were shooting at. I couldn't understand why they were shooting at their own planes. The airplane turned every possible way to show its emblem. I kept quiet. The airplane exploded in fire. I said to myself, one less airplane in the battle against the Americans.

After the airplane exploded in fire the soldiers realized that they had made a mistake. The Lieutenant came storming outside. I said to myself, I had better get inside quickly and stay out of trouble.

But when I went inside, my mother was furious. She told me that I was impossible, that someday something horrible was going to happen to me.

I replied, "But mamma, I was washing clothes."

She retorted, "You think you can't die because you are washing clothes?" With all the shooting of the cannons and the airplanes, our house was suffering the consequences. Tiles were falling off the roof. The glass windowpanes were cracking. And then one day, all the glass in the windows flew out. I found a cardboard box. I cut pieces to the measured sizes. I started to use the hammer and nails to put the pieces of cardboard into the places where the windows had been. Then the shooting started. It was very bad. The force of the explosion blew the cardboard away and took the hammer from my hand. I badly injured my arm and for a couple of days I couldn't move my arm. At that moment, I was petrified. I ran into our room and cowered in the corner on the floor until the shooting was over.

At the shelter, everyone was busy. The men had almost finished the tunnel. One man was assigned to cut tobacco leaves to make cigarettes. The only paper that was available was newspaper. The men took turns making cigarettes. They picked the tobacco leaves in the field. They selected the ones that were getting brown. People planted tobacco in the Agro Romano. They also planted cotton.

Finally the shelter was finished. There was a celebration. I brought the food for everybody. There was now more room for all the people in the shelter.

I returned home and told Mamma and Papa. They also were very glad.

It was January 1943 and the very next morning as everyone was getting out of the shelter, they saw a little German truck with big antennae near the entrance of the shelter. We were told to leave, to go away. No one wanted to believe it.

Meanwhile at our house, we had just put the bread in the oven to cook. A German officer called my father. He told my father that everybody had to leave in five minutes. My father started to cry and said the bread was just in the oven to cook. If we left now, we would have no food for the children. The officer replied that there was not time for the cooking. My father cried—"Please we need the bread."

But the German officer insisted that we had to leave.

When the Germans chased us out of our house, my father pulled my mother aside.

"We have a dangerous thing to do. I have to get the prosciutto that we have saved in the double roof of the shed."

My mother asked my father if he was crazy.

"Leave it there! The Germans are there. They sleep there, they won't let you in."

"We need that prosciutto to cook with. There is not much oil left. I am going to get it. May God help me!"

My father took a ladder and called the camerati.

"I need to get into the room in the roof. I have to get something." The Germans let him in, and looking at him while talking to each other, they seemed to be asking one another what my father was doing. My father pulled the prosciutto out of its hiding place and made a sign to the Germans that he would split it with them. The Germans told him there was no need to share, because they had missed it the first place. They told Papa to leave.

When my father, armed with the prosciutto, met up with my mother, he was still trembling. "I had a funny feeling that something would happen to me. Thank God the way things turned out."

The prosciutto was just fine and we put it to good use. We put it in the wagon. At that moment, another officer with lots of medals on his lapel approached us. He had spoken to Papa a few days earlier and had told him that he was from Poland.

He asked my father why he was running. My father told him what happened. He turned to that officer yelling in German. The officer put his hand to salute the Polish officer. The Polish officer told the other officer to leave. He patted my father on the shoulder and said, "You can stay until the bread is cooked. Everyone else will leave in five minutes. Just hurry.

I can't describe what went on. I ran out to the shelter yelling.

"Hurry, hurry! We have to leave in five minutes. We have no time for anything."

Everyone was trying to decide what to do. The word was passed through out the shelter. Bring the food; take the cow that has milk. Take a blanket for each family. We had to take care to grab our personal valuables. The wagon was for food. We hung some kettles under the wagon.

We got everything we could and we formed a caravan. We began to leave. It was in the afternoon and we agreed to meet at the cross roads by the Gentile house. We put some straw in the big room on the floor to make beds. We organized our belongings. And that was when my father caught up with us with the cooked bread.

Before it got dark, the canons began to shoot. Everybody ran into the Gentile's house. We were lucky because a big piece of the house fell in the courtyard making a big hole in the ground. This was not to far from the door. The shell was smoking and we were afraid it would explode. It kept on smoking until the next morning. We thanked God for our safety. Early the next morning, the shooting began again. Marco was with somebody on the second floor of the house near the window as shrapnel passed very near his head. The two men ran downstairs.

Everybody was busy getting ready. My father and my brother, along with Mr. Gentile were trying to hide some wheat under the big oven outside, using some bricks. Maria made a hole in the ground to put some things she had in a small hope chest. She covered it over like a tombstone and made a cross she found. She put a German helmet on the cross.

Rome
1944

IT was decided that we would go to Rome. We hoped God would guide us.

About 10 A.M. while everybody was busy, we heard lots of noise on the road. We went outside to see what it was and it was a caravan like ours. A woman was crying in the front of the caravan. Her children were on the others side, in front with the Americans. These people had been chased by the Germans and wanted help. We told them we needed to help ourselves. We explained that we were 45 people and that all of them, could not join us. They said thanks and asked the good Lord to help us all.

Before eleven in the morning, the caravan started heading toward Rome. We were not far from a place called Divino Amore named for the Madonna. Airplanes came with machine guns, shooting. Everybody fell to the ground. There was a bridge nearby. Marco and another young man said. "We will see if it will be safe for us to stay under that bridge."

When the two returned, they warned all of us that the bridge was full of mines. I continued to stand up because I wanted to see what was going on. My mother was yelling at me to get down. "Do you want to die?" I went down on the ground.

When the shooting ended, everybody got together. We put our fear aside and again started walking toward Rome.

I looked back where the horse and wagon were and started to laugh. Maria asked me if I had gone crazy.

"No," I answered. "Just look at your husband!" Dario was wearing a cream trench coat. In order to escape from the shooting, he went under the wagon where we had hung the big kettle we made food in. The kettle was blackened from soot. The entire back of Dario's trench coat was black. I thought it was funny. I had told him not to go under the wagon since it was no safer than the ground. He just hadn't listened.

When we were not too far from Rome, we all stopped and started to talk, trying to figure out what to do. We could not stay all of us in one group. We decided to split up.

Our now smaller group stopped as we arrived at the road Appia Antica. It was almost dark. We saw a trattoria. We knocked at the door and the owner told us that the trattoria was closed. We all gathered around and pleaded with the owner. We had been walking since morning from Pomezia. We explained how the Germans had chased us out of our house. The owner opened his door to all fourteen in our group. We were two families. There were seven of us Di Tommaso, eight with Marco and the Gentile family had six people.

I do not remember what the owner cooked for us. He gave us some wine. We celebrated being alive. The owner apologized that all of us could not stay in his place, as it was too small. The Gentile family offered to leave. The owner suggested that they go to the house next door, which would have room.

My mother requested that I go with Mrs. Gentile. "Please Carmela, take Sonia with you. She has a temperature. I think she is having an attack of appendicitis."

Mrs. Gentile agreed. We went to the house next door and they gave us one room with only one bed. I lay on the floor, which was tiled. It was so cold and there were no covers. I could not sleep at all. When I remember that night, I can still feel the cold in my bones.

Early in the morning, we all got together. We found out that Marco and my brother Vincenzo slept in the garage in the truck. Marco had gotten sick on the wine from the night before and was having a hard time in the morning.

We regrouped and again agreed to separate the two families. The Gentile family went one way and we went another.

Mama and Papa decided to go along the Appia Antica. We passed the catacombs of St. Sebastiano. Not to far from that point, were the catacombs of St. Callisto. We saw a gate there. There were priests across the street and there was a big house surrounded by a big brick wall. At the door, there was a stone plank saying "Villa Sgaravatti." My father stood amazed. He told us the house belonged to the company from which he bought seed for our farm.

Mama and Papa looked at each other and then walked up to the house and rang the bell. A lady came to answer the bell. She talked to Mama and Papa. Then she opened the gate for us and it was like entering the Garden of Eden.

The garden was full of beautiful flowers. There were lots of Irises and many other flowers. There was a big yard and a big pig pen. The housekeeper told us that we could stay here. The Sgaravatti family would not return before the summer.

The housekeeper had a family. They had their own apartment. I do not remember her name but her husband's name was Signor Giovanni. There were two daughters, Marianna and Savina and a little boy who was retarded. Even today we thank God for leading us to that place. We had come to a safe place.

Before we had left Pomezia, my father had put some grain in the wagon. We found a mill to crush the grain and to make the flour for the bread and the pasta.

Across from the Villa at the Catacombs of St. Callisto, there was a caretaker with the family. They took care of the entrance and the house for the priests. We met the caretakers and they told us they had a big oven to cook the bread and that we could use it as long as we provided the wood. My mother agreed and she told all of us children to go and find some wood on the land that was not too far from the garden. We went to find the wood for the fire.

The first time we made the bread and it was finished, we put the bread on a pasta board. We were crossing the street when a man approached us and said to my mother, "Lady, are you crazy?"

My mother asked him what he was talking about.

"If people see you with the bread, they are going to assault you and take all the bread. Do you know how lucky you are that you have flour? People are starving."

After that we kept the bread in a sack when we came out from the baking place, we would first check to make sure no one was coming.

One day, someone knocked at our door and my mother asked who it was.

A man's voice said, "Please, Signora, I have something I want to tell you."

His voice was trembling. My mother opened the door and asked the man how she could help him.

"Signora, someone told me that you make bread. I implore you: when you sift your flour, don't throw away what is left. When the flour is separated, may you give it to me what you would discard? I have three children and I have nothing to feed them. My mother was about to cry. She told the man to return the day after tomorrow and she would give him what he asked for. She then gave him a loaf of bread

The next day when I was sifting the flour for the bread, my mother told me to leave a little bit of flour so that the man could put it together to make some kind of bread for his family. She reminded me that they had to survive too.

When the man came, he kissed my mother's hands and said that our Lord would reward her. He came every week until Rome was liberated from the Germans and we left to return to Pomezia.

Our supply was going down as well. My mother, father and I wondered how we could get the wheat that we had left home under Mr. Gentile's oven. We had no transportation. Signore Giovanni, the villa keeper, said he would see what he could find. One night, he called my father and said he had found a way to get what he need. He knew someone who had a truck.

"But it will cost you," Signore Giovanni told my father. "And someone has to go with the driver. You know the driver has to go where the battle is and his life is in jeopardy."

My father directed Signore Giovanni to find out when they could leave. That night, we had a big meeting to decide who was going.

"I have to go to the Gentile's to find out who is going with whoever we send from out family," my father said.

My brother Vincenzo was a young man. We were afraid the Germans would get him. I volunteered.

"Sonia," my mother said, "as always you have no fear. I don't know if it is a good idea for you to go alone. Someone else has to go."

Marco spoke up. "I'll go with her."

"No Marco, you cannot go. The Germans will get you as soon as they see you."

"No, they won't." Marco responded. "I'll show my card and I'll say that I belong to the Republica di Salo."

And so it was decided that Marco would go from our family. When my father spoke with Signor Gentile, he agreed to make the arrangements. He said he would determine who would be going from the Gentile family.

The Gentile family decided that their daughter Annetta and her son Mario would come.

So it was that Marco and I volunteered from the Di Tommaso family, Annetta and Mario from the Gentile family.

The next day, the man with the truck came early in the morning to pick us up. We then went to the Gentile to pick up Annetta and Mario. As we left the Appia Antica road, we drove out of town on the road called Laurentina. We could hear the battle as it raged toward Ardea Nettuno, which is near Anzio.

The four of us were worried. We started to sing to lift our spirits, joking that if we die, we did do so singing.

When we finally reached my home, the Germans came out with their guns pointing at us. I started to say loudly as I came out of the truck, "Don't shoot!!! I am Sonia Di Tommaso!!! Call Peter!! Call Peter!!"

Finally Peter came out of the house. He was the Polish young man who was fighting with the Germans. He and I had become friends during my time at the house. He spoke some Italian and he stopped the soldiers from shooting us. I explained that we had returned to get something that we needed.

As quickly as we could, we went to get the wheat. We got as much as we could get as we hurriedly moved the bags.

Peter came out and told me that it was a good thing that we had come when we did. He said the Germans had been under serious fire the day before and during the night. They had lost a few soldiers. He soon left, as he couldn't spend any more time talking to us.

With the wheat in the truck, we left the house and went to the crossroads at the Gentile's home. We hoped to find the wheat we had hidden under the oven. We saw that the bricks were still there. We broke the wall and saw the burlap bags full of wheat. We looked at each other and thanked God that we had found what we needed to have. As quickly as we could, we loaded the wheat and left before something might happen to us. We were soon on the road to Rome.

When we got back, there were no words to describe how happy both of the families were. We divided the wheat between the two families and paid the driver with money and wheat.

"To tell you the truth," the driver said, "I did not think it would have been so dangerous. I went because you promised me some wheat beside the money. Don't call me again! I wouldn't do it for all the money in the world!"

The truck driver left and we never saw him again.

As the days and weeks went by, all the young people got together: My brother Vincenzo, Antoine, Marco, and me, as well as the daughters of the couple who took care of the Villa Sgarvatti, Savina and Marianna. Also with us was Teresina, the daughter of the people who took care of the Selesian priests' house. Other young people came from a few houses away. One of them brought a gramophone with records and suggested that we go into the field away from the road. We took the gramophone and the records and went to the field where we set things up near a big tree. Two other boys were with Teresina. I asked who they were as I hadn't seen them before.

"I will tell you if you promise me, before God, you will not tell anybody else," Teresina said.

Of course, we all promised to God and to her that we would not tell anyone. She told us the boys were Jewish, that they were staying with her family and with the priests, that only the priests and her family knew they were Jewish. Their father was an officer in the Italian army and he came to hide his sons from the Germans. The boys joined in with the makeshift celebration in the field and we all had a good time. We all took turns turning the gramophone.

Later, when we went to mass, the two boys came with us, although they did not make the sign of the cross.

Marco came with us once in awhile. Usually he left every morning so we did know where he went. But later we found out. One day the airplane attacking and cannon sounds, intensified. Marco was preparing to leave and both my mother and father stopped him.

"Marco," my father said, "we never asked you where you are going because you are old enough to make your own decisions. But today the shooting is very bad. We do not want you to go out."

"I have to go!" Marco replied.

"No Marco!" my mother said. "You cannot go!"

Marco turned and looked at both of them. "You have to promise me not to tell a soul what I am going to tell you. I am working for the underground with the Allies. I have an appointment with a general today. I have no choice — I must go."

We were all stunned by what he told us. Marco had been stopped once before. If he were apprehended with the general, both would be taken to Via Tasso and tortured for information. We promised to tell no one.

"God be with you." my mother said and began to cry.

From that day on, each day that Marco went out we all waited anxiously for him to come home. One day two men in civilian clothes stopped him. They asked him questions. He showed them a card with his photo indicating that he was a police officer. They let him go, but he was afraid they would take him when he went home.

Marianna and Savina, the caretaker's daughters, at the Villa

"Thank God, I made it home," he said after he was questioned.

The same week that happened, I was in the hospital Santo Spirito across the bridge. The bridge is called Sant' Angelo be-

Marco and Baby Dino at the villa

cause the Castle Sant' Angelo is across the River. I was there being operated for appendicitis. I could not stand the pain any
longer, as the attacks were coming more and more often. While I

was being operated on, I heard the doctor say, "Look she is awake. We need to give her more chloroform."

"No, I said, no, no, no! I will not move, I will not move!"

The sirens were starting to go off, warning people to move into the shelters. The doctor finished the operation without giving me more chloroform. The next day when my mother came to the hospital to see me, the doctor said, "Signora, your daughter is very lucky that you brought her to be operated on. Her appendix was very bad. If she had another attack, it might have burst and she could have died."

I was in the hospital for one week and then I went home.

One night, we were all in the kitchen talking. Suddenly, we heard some noise outside. It sounded like a cry. My father said he would go outside alone to see what was happening.

My father told all the men in the kitchen to get out of the house and go hide in the pig pen. When they were all gone, my father opened the door. A German soldier was in the street crying in pain. My father went to him and brought him inside our house. His ankle was horribly swollen. My mother started to get something to help when we heard a loud pounding at the front door. The door was shaking.

My father opened the front door and four Germans soldiers entered, their guns pointing at all of us, ready to shoot. We all raised our arms and started crying. The Germans turned their attention to my father. I heard the soldier who was injured crying. I wanted to help but the soldiers with the guns were very angry.

They pointed their guns at my father. "You have done a very bad thing," one of the solders said to him. "You helped a deserter."

Apparently, the wounded solder had jumped out of truck and had come to our place for help.

The Germans with the guns told my father that he would have to carry the wounded deserter to the hospital on the Appia Antica, a distance of about two kilometers, near Cecilia Metella. This was the closest German hospital.

Marco, under cover at Villa Sgaravatti,
leaving to meet with his superiors

My father picked up the wounded soldier on his back and the entire party set off for the hospital. The rest of us were just praying that nothing would happen to my father. We were afraid that the Germans would keep him or send him somewhere and we would not see him again. We knew that the Germans were sending men into Siberia. And, in the view of the Germans, my father had committed a very bad offense.

We were so grateful to God when he came home several hours later. Not too long after that incident, my father told my mother that he had to go somewhere with the horse and wagon,

"Where do you have to go?" my mother asked.

"I will tell you when I come home. I have to go now and do somebody a favor." He kissed my mother and then he said he would see us all later.

After several hours, he came back. He looked very pale and upset. "Where did you go?" My mother asked. "What happened"?

"I had no idea it would be so dangerous," my father said. "Where did you go?" my mother asked again.

"You know those two Jewish boys that are hiding across the street with the Salesian priests? Their father was an officer in the Italian army, or so we were told. He and his family were in hiding. He asked me to do him a favor. He explained that it had to be done at once. He gave me an address where I was to pick up a trunk and bring it back to him. He told me exactly where it was. My father kept a horse and cart at the monastery and used them to pick up the trunk.

"When I got to the place, I realized how great the danger was. The location was under surveillance by the Germans! And, thanks to our Lord, nobody saw me go inside the building. I went inside, got the trunk and took it to the Jewish Colonel. He was waiting at the gate and didn't even say thank you as he was running away."

The next day, the entire family was gone and we never found out where they went or if they survived.

I have done some research on this subject. I found out that Keppler, a leader of the Roman Gestapo, demanded 50 kilograms of gold[1] from Ugo Foa and Dante Almansi,[2] two leaders of the Jewish community in order to let the Roman Jews leave Rome.

---

[1] *Mussolini and the Jews*, pg. 355, Michaelis, 1978.
[2] Ibid.; *Italians and the Holocaust*, pg. 106, Zuccotti, 1987.

Sitting from left, Teresina, me, Savina and Lena at the Villa

He demanded the gold be delivered in 36 hours. I speculate that my father may have been the part of the chain of events to deliver the gold.

The girls with the Jewish boys at Sgaravatti

My father risked his life that day, he came home terrified, but God helped him. We were very glad that our father had not been caught by the Germans and was still with us.

On June 22, 1944, my mother told us we had to go to the center of Rome

"I need two of you because we have to go and wait on long lines to get the stamps for food."

As usual, I volunteered. Marco said he would go along as well.

On June 23, the three of us, left the house and walked along the Appia Antica until we came to the Arch of Saint Sebastiano. Near there we were able to take the trolley. When we got off the trolley, we had to take a bus to where we could collect the stamps for the food. As we approached the Piazza Colonna, the bus was about to stop. We could see from the window a German column passing by. We were almost at the center of the Piazza, when a violent explosion occurred. Everyone on the bus started

*Me, left, and Savina in the Iris fields at Villa Sgaravatti.
The Irises were given to the Allied liberators as they passed by*

yelling "don't stop the bus, keep going, Run! Fast." We heard more big explosions and shooting. People outside the bus were running. Everyone on the bus ducked under the seats of the bus. Mamma, Marco and I were on the floor. The passengers on the bus soon realized that we were all in great danger. We screamed at the bus driver, telling him to get the bus moving and get us out of there. He hurriedly started the bus and drove away.

What was happening in the Piazza was horrifying. People were screaming, the German soldiers were shooting. The bus driver kept on going. He stopped far away, about two stops from the Piazza. He opened the door and we all got off the bus at a safe distance from the Piazza.

We all ran away from the bus. Eventually, we reached our destination, finished our errands and then went home, getting back much later than we expected.

When we got home, the rest of our family was relieved, as they had been worried about us. They all asked what had happened to us. We told them that we were lucky to be in the bus and how we got off and ran. People in the Piazza Colonna and the
the surround area didn't know what was happening. The next day, we had heard that not far from where we lived, a tremendous noise like a bomb, exploded. It was clear to all of us that something bad was happening.

Every night a boy, his name was Italo Casale, would come to our house to get a container of milk. We were helping a friend of our brother-in-law Dario, Claudio Casale. Claudio was the dean of the school. He and his wife had a baby also, Italo's little brother. There were eight children in the house. The night of the explosion near our house, Italo came very late. We asked him why he was so late.

"I had to go from Via Delle Sette Chiese which is near the Fosse Ardeatine." Italo told us. "Then I crossed the Catacombs of Santo Callisto and then came here.

He said there were lots of Germans with guns. They would not permit Italo to go through. He had to go the long way to our place.

The next night he was late again. "I came from the place I usually do but tonight there was a bad odor. I could barely breathe."

Gate and Statue memorial to the Ardeatine Massacre

"I wondered what was going on yesterday when the Germans would not let me go the usual way," he added.

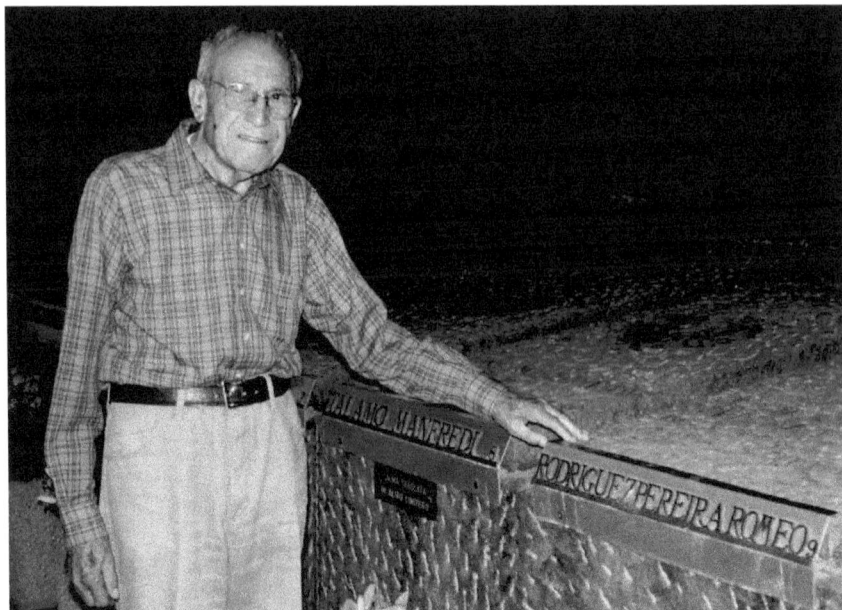

Marco was very moved after visiting the grave
of his friend and fellow officer at Fosse Ardeatine

The following day, his father met with Dario. He told Dario that something big must have happened past the wall of the Salesian priests to make the Germans prevent Italo from going through.

After that day we found out that when we were in the bus at Piazza Colonna, the Germans took everyone that were in the Piazza and in the surrounding houses, into custody. The Germans did this in retaliation because of a column of German soldiers had been bombed and thirty-two of them had been killed. The Germans took ten Italians for every German and they shot each one of them.

When the Germans gathered up the people from the Piazza, they did not have enough. So, they went to the prison, Regina Coeli, and gathered up as many as they wanted. In total, 335 Italians were killed. The bad smell was the rotting bodies.

When we found out what had happened we all went down on our knees and thanked God that he had inspired us to get the bus driver to drive on. Had the bus stayed at Piazza Colonna, the Germans would have taken us as well.

Much later, we found out that the names of the German officers that made the decision to kill all the Italians in retaliation for the loss of the German soldiers. General Kessingler and General Malzer, officers in the German army, were responsible for the killings.

Today in that place, Fosse Ardeatine, there is a mausoleum with the names of those who were murdered, carved in stone.

One of those murdered was Marco's captain. In fact, he was one of the first ten to be killed. His name was Rodriguez Romeo Pereira.

At Villa Sgaravatti, all of us were helping one another. In a house not too far from us, the people were hiding another German deserter. Everybody took turns feeding him. Most of the time, he hid in the Catacombs of San Callisto, especially during the daylight hours.

Marco would go visit him in the Catacombs and they would talk. One day, the deserter told Marco to follow him. He made Marco understand that there were places he had not yet explored. He took Marco to a place where there was stream of water running. The two of them had to walk on their hands and knees. Marco told us that he was afraid the German would leave him there. The German had told Marco that sometimes when he saw the German couriers on motorcycles, he knew they had special orders to deliver, the deserter would stop them and take them into the Catacombs and leave them there. He told Marco he never killed them but they never came out because if someone went into the catacombs without a guide, they would never find their way out of the labyrinth.

Even today, if you go with a guide in the explored area, you need to stay with the guide the entire time.

During the German occupation of Rome, the Italian Partisans were fighting to regain our city. Many of the Partisans were getting killed. Marco continued to jeopardize his life.

The situation was getting worse and worse. We used to go in a field in the back of the villa. There was a wooded area and a meadow where we went with the gramophone to listen to music. We picked wild chicory, endive, thistle and other greens from the ground. My mother cooked them for dinner. She still made pasta but our flour supplies were dwindling.

My shoes were getting old.

"Look at my shoes!" I said to Mamma. "They have holes. What are we going to do? We'll see," my mother said.

She began to ask around if anyone knew where she could find an open market. She learned that there was such a market at Porta Portese. The next day mother told me that we would go there to see if we could find a pair of shoes.

When we took the tram, we sat close together and held onto each other remembering the shooting in the Piazza Colonna. When we reached Porta Portese, we walked around and finally we found a stand with shoes for sale. There were not too many choices but we managed to find a black pair that fit me. These were not leather, but we bought them anyway.

I was so happy to have a new pair of shoes but the happiness didn't last long. One day when I was out in the rain with my new shoes, I started walking and my shoes came apart. They were made of sawdust! I started to cry.

I had to take them off. When I went home my mother asked me why I was crying.

"Mamma ... look at my shoes!" I said as I showed them to her.

"What are we going to do!" my mother said. "I cannot believe this. We have no more stamps to buy you more shoes."

I was thinking about this problem. I remembered I saw some farmer's shoes which were made of wood.

"Mamma," I said, "I could make the bottom souls out of wood, and use some rags for the top of the shoes."

"We will see," my mother said. "Perhaps we can ask Savina's mother if we might use her sewing machine." Savina's mother was the villa's caretaker.

We finally found what I needed and made myself a pair of sandals that I could wear and walk in.

Around this time, my sister's baby Dino was getting bigger. He started to get sick. He began to have convulsions and he would stop breathing and turn blue. There were no doctors around. My mother knew lots of home remedies. She told Maria to hurry up and put Dino in a basin with cold water. That helped each time he had a convulsion. After a while, he grew out of having them and became a very healthy baby. To this day he is a very healthy man.

As time passed, the battle in Anzio was raging. The Allies were bombing Monte Cassino almost every day. We got the news from people that delivered wine from Castelli Romani using a horse and carriage. These people were the only ones that were willing to take a chance to come to Rome. We asked them why no one came with food to sell. We were told the sellers didn't come because there was no food to sell.

The Germans were getting weaker. They were moving from one location to another.

One day my brother Vincenzo came to my mother. "Mamma, Mamma! Signor Giovanni (the caretaker) told me the Germans are leaving Forte Boccea tomorrow morning. They are leaving things behind. I want to go and see if I can find something useful."

"No, I am afraid that the Germans might still be there." Mamma said. "We know what the Germans are like when we lived at home."

"Mamma, Signor Giovanni is older than you. You know him, he is telling the truth."

"Okay," Mamma said, so the next morning, Vincenzo, and Signor Giovanni, left very early.

Forte Boccea was far from where we lived. It was near Via Trionfale near the Palatino, which is the hospital, almost 15 kilometers away.

Later that afternoon, we saw my brother Vincenzo and Signor Giovanni returning, each had a big bag on their shoulders.

"We didn't find any food but we did find German uniforms," my brother said. "With this material, you girls can do some sewing!"

As they put the bags of uniforms on the ground, my mother opened one of the bags and screamed.

"My God! Look at this! It is infested with lice! What are we going to do with it now?"

Mamma first insisted that we had to bury the uniforms in order for all of us not to become infested. But then she decided she would try to salvage the material. She told me to get the big kettle that we use to boil the water to do the laundry. She also told me to get some wood, light a fire under the kettle full of water and when the water was hot, mamma figured she would put the uniforms in the water to boil for awhile.

Mamma told Signor Giovanni and my brother Vincenzo about the lice. Both of them understood what they had to do. My brother got undressed behind the bushes. Mama told him that she would give him hot water to wash himself. She also instructed them to give us their clothes.

So we boiled the clothes and uniforms and got rid of the lice. The next day we dried the uniforms and Mamma tried to figure out what to do with them. She figured that if she could get some navy blue dye, we could dye them and use the fabric to make us coats. Mama wondered which one of us needed a coat the most.

A few days later it was June 4. Early in the morning, we heard loud noises on the Appia Antica. This was the first road the Romans made of cobblestone and the oldest street in Rome. The sound was loud and harsh. We peaked over the wall of the Villa and we saw Germans walking towards the Arch of Sant. Sebastiano. We called our father and told him to come in a hurry to see what was happening.

My father came and watched the Germans. He said, it looked like the Germans are retreating. We all got behind the wall and stood by the gate, where we could see. The line of German soldiers was horrible to watch. Many of the soldiers were injured, some of them bleeding from open wounds. Some soldiers could barely walk. All the soldiers were leaning on sticks. There were wounded horses with flesh hanging from their backs.

Some of the soldiers couldn't walk anymore and they tried to sit on the ground to rest. Other soldiers yelled at them to keep on going. The line of the retreating and injured soldiers seemed to stretch forever. Every time I think of that day, my stomach still gets knotted up. The line began to diminish in the late afternoon. Finally, the Germans were gone.

About five minutes after the last German soldier had moved beyond our site, we heard more noises, loud noises. My God, are they coming back, I wondered?

We looked outside and saw tanks. We soon realized that these were not German tanks but American tanks.

We opened the big gate. The tanks stopped in front of the villa.

"Ben venuti! Ben venuti!" we all were yelling. "Welcome, welcome!!" We ran to the garden where there were lots of flowers, especially irises. We picked them all. What a memorable moment that was for all of us. We were so happy to see the soldiers with their tanks full of flowers. Some of the soldiers had movie cameras and were taking pictures. I am sure that those pictures are somewhere in the United States.

The next day, Marco said goodbye to all of us and thanked us for everything we had done for him. He went back to Via Delle Milizie, in Rome, where police headquarters were. He came back two days later. He had been transferred to Terni in the region of Umbria.

The war was still going on in northern Italy. The Germans were still fighting. They were still arresting Italians and killing them.

Tre Cannelle, Italy

A S for us, we were getting ready to go to Pomezia and to return to Tre Cannelle, to see our home. My father and mother decided to wait for a couple of days in case the Allies were on the road. We would have to walk on the same roads. We waited for three days until we started our journey. As we passed the big walls of Rome, we saw ammunitions everywhere. The Germans had left in a great hurry. We saw rifles standing up in a triangle, just left behind. We were walking through an abandoned battleground. The smell of gunpowder was still in air. It was such a terrible sight that I will never forget.

As we approached our town, things got even worse. After walking for many hours, we approached our neighborhood and we saw such destruction. Houses had no roofs. We were very anxious to see if our house was still standing.

When we finally got to our home, we saw only four walls. As we approached the kitchen door, we saw a mound of dirt. The German soldiers had made a shelter that went underground from the center of kitchen. On the second floor, I could see the sky. Only one of the upstairs rooms still had a roof. Downstairs, the room where my mother, father and I had stayed in was still intact. We went to see the stable and that was not too bad. We inspected the outside of the house. We looked at the oven where we bake the bread and that was still standing. Right then, we said, thank God.

My father decided to see if the papers he had hid for the police station had survived the war. He climbed onto the roof and removed the bundle of papers. He returned them, to the police station.

Around the outside of the house there was ammunition and spent shells. In a ditch not too far from the house were fuses. It looked like black spaghetti. In fact, later my brothers Vincenzo,

Antoine and I would play by lighting up one end and quickly throw in on the ground. The ammunition would jump as it exploded. We used to see which one of us could throw the lighted explosive the farthest. When my mother saw what we were doing, she scolded us.

"You better be careful!!" she said, "We have better things to do for our home than to blow it up completely!!"

But the explosives were everywhere. One day as I was walking around the house, I saw something that I thought was very interesting to me. I said to myself, I wonder what it is. It was a little ball and it was very heavy. I started to pull out all the screws and at a certain point, powder came out. At that moment, my father appeared.

"What are you doing?" he asked. "Are you crazy?!?"

He slapped me. He had never done that before and he said to me, "Do you realize what you have done?" This is a grenade and you just dismantled it. You are very lucky it did not explode!"

I later learned it was an American grenade. When my father died, I found a box in his room. In it, was my first painting, rolled up in a newspaper and the grenade that I had dismantled and a shell casing. When I saw them in that box, I started to cry. My father kept it in his room until he died.

"Look what I found in this box!" I said to my sister, Maria.

"Papa never forgot the miracle of this grenade that it never exploded in your hand. You could have been killed."

I still have that box with the grenade and the shell casing inside. I have them in my home in America.

After awhile, everybody started to work to clear out the kitchen. At least we could start to cook some food in it.

All the men in the neighborhood got together with my father and they all began searching for their belongings that were scattered around. The men set off in different directions. One person decided to go to the grove where the cork trees grew, sughereto. After awhile, everyone had gone his or her separate ways when we heard yelling from one man in the grove. He called for all of us to come and see what he had found. Everybody in the vicinity ran to the corkwoods. When they got there, they saw all of our belongings tied onto the trees. My mother's sewing machine was on the tree, as were lots of our other belongings. Also hanging on the tree were the remains of a person who had tried to claim the items for himself. He hung on the tree in pieces, having been blown up by a mine because the Germans booby trapped the trees. As we looked over the trees, we could see mines everywhere. We had to leave our belongings hanging there until someone from the military could come and take away the mines.

With little to work with, we all had to improvise. Somehow we refashioned the kitchen and we were able to make bread. There was not much else available to eat. We went into the fields and searched for what we knew was edible. We found chicory and other greens. The American soldiers also gave us some food and we always grateful to them for what they did for us. One soldier from Pennsylvania was able to send a letter from us to Marco's father in Brooklyn. Somehow I came to understand that we all had to learn to survive until everybody in town came back and life would begin once again.

One day after the dough for the bread was made and had begun to rise, Mama told me to start the fire in the oven. I went out and I started the fire. Nearby, there was a big rock and I sat down on it. All of a sudden, I felt something crawling all over me. I looked down and I could see hundreds of lice were crawling on me. I started to scream and my mother came running.

"Mamma, Mamma!" I screamed, "Look, look at these bugs!"

When she came closer to me and saw that I was full of lice, she called out to God.

"Go somewhere where nobody can see you and take off your clothes," she said. She gave me a big rag and a small one. She told me to scrub with the small rag until all the lice were off me. Then I was to cover myself with the big rag until she got the water warm.

"Then we will do what we did at the Villa in Rome," she instructed—we would boil my clothes!

After Mamma took care of me, she burned the ground all around the house. Meanwhile the bread became sour dough because it stood long after it had risen. We ate it anyway as we had no alternative.

As we settled into our house, my sister Maria, her husband, Dario and baby Dino went to live in the school in Pomezia. They had one room. The school was still standing but in was in bad shape. Dario and Maria explained that they could not stay with us because with the house so damaged, there was not enough room.

"We will manage," Dario said. "And I have to see what all we have to do re-open the school."

Soon after he and Maria and Dino departed, he was successful in reopening the school. He and Maria had one more son who was born in the school. Two more sons came later after the family had moved out of the school.

When finally everybody came back to the town, they elected Dario mayor of Pomezia. He was the first mayor of the town. Before he was elected, Pomezia was under the town hall of Rome. He was also the longest continuous teacher in the school, having taught for 41 years.

Dario died February 26, 2005. Many of the students he taught in the town came to his funeral. Many tears were shed. Dario was proclaimed to be a brave man. His casket was placed in the council chamber so that all the people of Pomezia could see the first great mayor of their city.

Marco was stationed in Terni. He came to see us and told us that his father had sent a letter in response to the letter the soldier from Pennsylvania had mailed for us. Can anybody imagine the joy of Marco's father in Brooklyn, New York, USA receiving a letter saying simply, "Papa, I am alive!"

Marco's parents also wrote to my parents, thanking them for saving his life. It was a very touching letter and it made all of us in the family cry.

Later, when Marco went to Sicily, his mother and his sisters could not believe their eyes that it was Marco. His brother came home by way of Calabria because he was stationed in Calabria but also could not take a chance that he might be killed in crossing the Strait of Messina.

Marco and me on our Wedding Day, April 11, 1948

A few months later, Marco came back. He was coming from Civitavecchia, which was in the province of Lazio, not too far from Rome.

My parents asked him why he came back? They asked if he had a pass?

Marco responded that he could stay for a week. And then he explained.

"I came to Civitavecchia," Marco began, "to bring a company of carabinieri. They have been assigned to go north to fight. The objective was to chase the Germans out of our country. We were waiting for the warship to come to take the men to the front. Today we were told the war is over. The Germans are defeated. They surrendered and all the soldiers went home. The war ended on Aril 25, 1945. I can only stay a few days before I go back to Terni."

We all gathered around Marco and I said, "Say it again, say it again!!" "The war is over," Marco repeated.

We all started to jump up and down. Joy filled the house. We ran outside and started to yell, "The war is over!!" We called to our neighbors and gave them the good news.

For us, the war ended when the Allies came into Rome. The rest of countrymen were still suffering and dying for our country. We thanked God that the suffering was over and that now we could begin to rebuild our lives. This day was just the beginning.

During Marco's visit, he asked me to marry him.

"I love you, Sonia," he said to me. And I hope you love me. While I am here, you can give me the answer because I want to ask your mother and father for your hand."

I was stunned, shocked. I never expected Marco to ask me to be his bride. I loved Marco as I loved my brothers. I told him that.

"I have never had a boyfriend that I can compare you to."

He stopped me and he said, "I know this is true but I assure you, I will be your love."

Marco and Sonia on their First Anniversary, 1949

I told Marco to leave me for a while so that I could let the shock of his proposal wear off a little. He agreed and he went away.

That night at the dinner table, my mother asked me what was wrong with me, as I was not eating anything. I told her I had a headache. That night I could not sleep. I said to myself, I know Marco. He is a good person. We got along very well for all those months. We did lots of work together and we always agreed. We almost died together, when we left Rome, to get the Wheat. I will ask God to help me change the love of a brother to the love a woman for a man. And, that's what happened.

The next day I told him I was willing to marry him. I told him that we couldn't get married right away, that we would have to wait awhile. He agreed that we would wait. We both were in agreement and he told me he would tell my parents that night at dinner.

After we had finished the evening meal, I got up quickly and ran upstairs. I could still hear what was being said downstairs.

"I want to talk to both of you," Marco began. "What's wrong?" Mama asked worriedly.

"Nothing is wrong," Marco continued. "I would like to marry your daughter."

"Our daughter is married, you know that," my father said. "I want to marry Sonia," Marco said.

"She is just a child," my parents said at the same time.

"Yes, she is a child," Marco replied. We will wait until she is grown." I was 16 years old when I became engaged. The family was happy.

Soon after Marco asked me to marry him, he went on furlough to Sicily. There, he told his family and they were very happy with the news. He also wrote to his father in Brooklyn, New York, USA.

Not too long after our engagement, my parents received a letter of joy from Marco's father, Ambrogio Cucinotta. He wrote that his son could not have made a better decision and that "The daughter of the family that saved my son's life will be more than welcome into the Cucinotta Family." Lidia Evans and Family.

In a following letter, Marco's father told him that as soon as he felt better, he would begin the paper work for Marco to come to America.

The paperwork did get done and Marco was on the waiting list to go to America. But the list of potential emigrants was long and nobody could tell when Marco would get called to Palermo for his trip to America.

The following year, 1946, we received news from Marco's brother Santo who also lived in Brooklyn that their father had passed away. Santo asked my father to go to Messina and tell the bad news to their mother.

"We have to go," my mother said. She and my father decided we would tell Marco and then my mother, Marco and I would go to Messina. When we got there, I found it hard to describe the sorrow that engulfed that family as they realized they would never be reunited with their father again. Their world crumbled and their grief was great.

Soon after we returned from Messina, my father and I became ill. We both had a fever. We started to tremble. We discovered that we had malaria. There were no medicines. My father remembered from World War I that we needed to find some Lupini beans, a very bitter bean. You have to cook it and soak it for one week and then you can eat them. But we had to cook them and then drink the water they were cooked in when it cooled.

My father asked lots of people. He finally found them and mother cooked them. She let the water stay one night outside of the window. The next morning she prepared two glasses—one for my father and one for me. The stuff was unbearable to drink. The water was so bitter. But we had to swallow it down no matter what. We were getting goose bumps for over two weeks as we had to drink the stuff each morning. I would say to myself that I wished the dawn would not come so soon. But the fever continued every day. After two weeks, my father's fever began to lessen but mine did not.

An American soldier came to the house and he asked what had happened. When he found out we had malaria, he came with quinine. But the quinine did not help me. I was in bed for a month. I became delirious. My mother sent for the doctor. When he came, he told my parents that I was very ill. He cautioned my parents that if started throwing up, that they should take me to the Santo Spirito hospital, in Rome, immediately. Hopefully, they will be able to save her. He told my parents that I was in a coma.

Early the next morning, I began to throw up. My parents took me to the hospital. I never remembered the trip. When I was there, they gave me quinine and adrenaline injections, because my trembling was so bad. I could not breathe. Every day at the same time I was getting the trembling. I was in the hospital for two months.

The mosquito that had bitten me carried a very bad virus. When I was sent home, the doctors told me that they hoped that I would improve and I did.

When I was recovered, I found that every time I went outside, I was afraid of the mosquitoes. They would swarm around me. The water in the streams stagnated and was a breeding ground for the mosquitoes.

Before the Germans sent us away, we had good drinking water. Now, you didn't even want to go near the water—it was horrible. It stayed that way until the government and city of Pomezia started to clean up the water supply by killing the mosquitoes with DDT spray.

The government sent a specialist to dismantle the mines that were all over the place. We had to be very careful when we walked alongside the roads. Booby traps and mines were hidden underground and in the fields.

When everything was cleaned up including the area by the corkwoods, we all were allowed to get our belongings.

My sister Maria went to the spot where she had buried the little trunk. The trunk was there but it was empty. My mother's sewing machine came back home and she started to sew for us again.

The time steadily passed as I waited to get married. On April 11, 1948, Marco and I got married in Saint Benedict's, the only Catholic Church still standing in Pomezia. The walls were full of bullet holes as were many of the other surrounding building, serving to remind us all of the recent war years.

We were very happy when that day our lives were finally joined together. Yet, we all still mourned the passing of Marco's father, in America. Both of us understood that we had to make the best of it because life is not what we would want it to be but what we must come to accept.

Sezze Romano
1948

IN May 1948, Marco was transferred to a town called Sezze
Romano. It was up north, not too far from Rome. It was in
the province of Littoria, which is called, Latina today.

I was not allowed to go with him because I needed the government's approval. That approval came in 1949, and that's
when I went to live with my husband in the new town. It wasn't
a very big town and all the people were very friendly.

We were very happy. In 1950, I gave birth to our son,
Ambrogio that translates to Ambrose, in English. Marco was still
waiting to hear from the American embassy about his acceptance
into America.

In 1953, Marco's mother died. She never had the joy to see
her son leave Italy and be reunited with his family in America.

Marco received his visa in January 1954. He had to travel to
the American consulate in Palermo to get it. With his papers in
hand, Marco left Italy on January 10, 1954 with the ship,
Vulcania. It arrived at its first stop, Halifax, Nova Scotia, covered
in ice and four days later, arrived in New York harbor on January 18, 1954

I remember one of the letters Marco wrote to me when he
finally got to see the Statue of Liberty. He wrote that he had to
ask himself if what he was seeing was real, if he were really in
America? It was so hard for him to realize that he had finally
made it.

Marco didn't have to go to Ellis Island. In 1954, the government stopped the ordeal that formerly accompanied immigrants
to the United Sates. Very soon upon arriving, he was reunited
with his brother, Santo and his sister Frances and all of their
families.

Left, Uncle Emilio, my mother's brother;
my mother, with young Dino, my father, and two friends

Marco quickly found work as a carpenter in Canarsie, Brooklyn. As soon as he could, he put in his application for Ambrose and me to come to the United States. Back at that time, the law stipulated that your family could not come to US unless you were already there. There was a lot of red tape. It took a year and a half before Ambrose and I received our visas.

America
1955

MARCO had been busy making a home for us. He had rented an apartment in the basement of a house. Ambrose and I left Italy from Naples on May 1955 on the ship the Andrea Doria. It took us eight days to cross the ocean. On the morning of the eighth day, we sailed into New York Harbor.

When I saw the Statue of Liberty, I thanked God that at long last we had made it to America and to our American dream.

Ambrose was five years old when we came to America. By September he was six years old and he started school. He had picked up a lot of English from the children next door. I was happy to see his report card at the end of his first school year. He was promoted with the other children.

Ambrose was a good student. Upon completing junior high school, he was selected from 500 applicants to attend the High School of Art and Design in Manhattan. Later, he went to the School of Visual Arts, also in Manhattan.

Once Ambrose was in school, I began to look for things to do. My neighbor told me she was working in Manhattan and that she was about to retire. I told her that I didn't think I could go to Manhattan and still be able to care for Ambrose who needed me. The lady, who spoke Italian, said to me that I was ambitious and that I could do something I wanted and that she would help me with Ambrose until I got home from work.

I told her that she was very kind and I thanked her for her help. I even kissed her in gratitude. I found a dress factory four avenues from our home. I started to make dresses but three weeks later, the company ran out of work.

Certificate to the Patriot

N. A227647*

In the name of the Governments and the people of the United Nations,

we thank you Marco Cucinotta for having fought the enemy on the

battleground as a soldier, in the ranks of the Patriots, which were the

men that used the armies for the triumph of liberty, furnishing

defensive operations, performing sabotage, and giving military

information.

With their courage and dedication the Italian Patriots effectively

contributed to the liberation of Italy and the grand cause of

Liberty for mankind.

In the Italy reborn, the possessors of the testimony will be applauded

as patriots that fought for honor and liberty.

Cosigned   H. R. Alexander
Caruso   Supreme Commander
Head of the Patriots   of the Allied Forces
                                            Central Mediterranean

Our landlord told me that he knew a man who was a presser in Manhattan. He promised to speak with his friend. I made contact with the gentleman and he introduced me to his work place. Two days later I met Mr. Jimmy, the owner of the factory.

Jimmy gave me a dress to make which I finished. Mr. Jimmy looked it over. He said the dress wasn't bad but that I was too slow. Further, I had already joined the union, which was required at my first job.

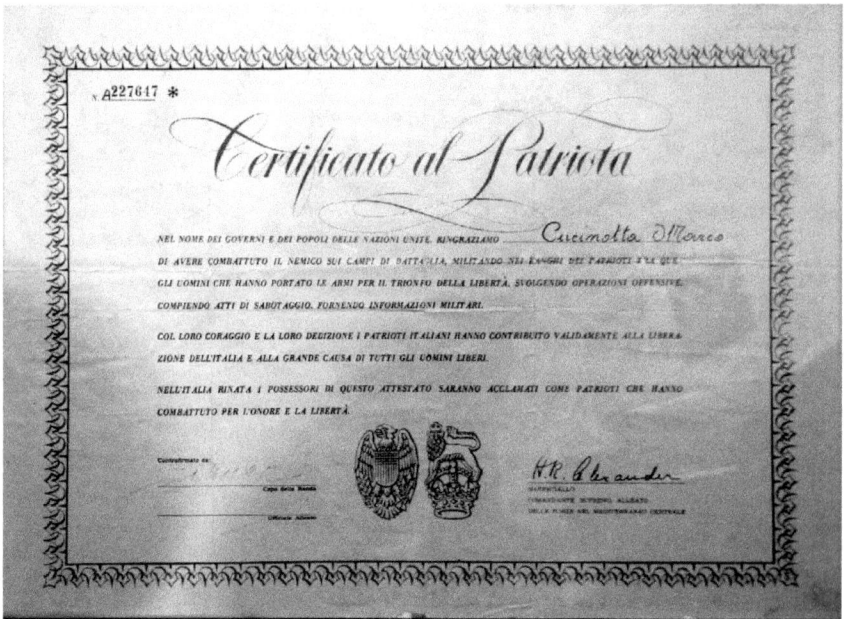

Certificate of Patriotism
signed from the Allied Forces Commander, Gen. Alexander

"If I give you work, I cannot fire you for two years after you start work and you are too slow. You need to be faster."

I started crying. "I have only been in this country for three months," I said through my tears. "You give me work and I promise you if you do not like how I do, you will not have to fire me. I will leave."

Mr. Jimmy spoke Italian. I worked for two weeks and then there was no more work.

"When I get more work," Mr. Jimmy said, I will tell Frank, the presser, and he will let you know when to come back."

Meanwhile, Marco's sister, Frances, told me there was a factory on 67th Street between 14th and 15th Avenues. At this time, we lived on 82nd Street. The factory was 15 blocks from our house. The next day, Frances came with me as we walked to the factory. We found the owner who also spoke a little Italian. His name was Charlie Pinta.

I explained to Mr. Pinta, that I had just come from Italy and that I need to find work. He looked at me.

Marco's Bullet Case

"This is the suit that we are making now," he said.

I replied that I thought it looked pretty complicated.

Mr. Pinta looked at me again. "I see in your eyes that you are not stupid. We have an Italian foreman that can help you if you need it. Come tomorrow morning and we will have work for you to do."

I came back the next day. They gave me the suit to be made. It was like a puzzle, probably seventy pieces. But I put everything together. They put it on the model figure and Mr. Pinta liked the work I had done.

"This dress fits well and so does the jacket," Mr. Pinta said. "I told you that you would be a good operator."

The company was called Leonard Arkin and it sold high-end garments. In one week I earned three times the money I had made in Manhattan. Three weeks after I had started, Mr. Jimmy sent word that I should go back to work. I told the presser to show the envelope indicating my earnings Mr. Jimmy. I also told the presser to tell Mr. Jimmy thanks but that I preferred to stay in Brooklyn.

My Original Passport

In a short time, I was making the samples to send to fit on the models for Leonard Arkin Company.

We found an apartment on 71st Street and 15th Avenue. This was closer to Ambrose's school so that I could go home and be with him at lunchtime. This apartment was also closer to my work so I didn't have to walk so many blocks.

Città di Pomezia

65° ANNIVERSARIO
Citta' di Pomezia
1939 - 2004

*Il Sindaco
On. Stefano Zappalà*

*Pomezia, 65th Anniversary plaque,
celebrating the rebuilding of Pomezia*

About this time, Marco changed jobs because there was no union and the company made cheap products. Marco was a fine craftsman and the place where he was working did not pay him for his skills. We discussed the issue and we both decided that Marco should try to see what other jobs might be available to him.

Now that I was earning some money, we both felt that Marco could take some time to find a job that would suit him. As it turned out, Marco did take some time. He met the son-in-law of our local grocer. Marco discussed with his situation and the level of his carpentry skill.

The man explained to Marco that he needed a sponsor to get into the carpenters union and the man offered to sponsor Marco at his union. It was in this manner that Marco joined the Carpenters Union. He worked in that trade up until his retirement after 50 years of working. He earned a 50 year pin in honor of his retirement.

Festa del Grano Medals

We both worked very hard and sacrificed a lot to be able to put money aside. We tried to pay for everything in cash, as we believed the interest we earned on our savings was making good money for us so we could buy a house. It takes of a lot of sacrifices to get enough money together to buy a house.

After seven years of working, we achieved our dream of home ownership and bought a house on West 4th St. in Brooklyn. It was a two family house. We figured we would rent the upstairs apartment to help pay for the house. When we went to close on the house, the owner asked us how we managed to put so much money together during the short time we were in America.

"I am born in this country," the owner said, "and I didn't have as much as this."

"If you went through the war as we did," I answered; you learn how to sacrifice and how to achieve your dreams just like we are doing today."

War mementoes, that were saved by my father before he died.
He kept them rolled up in newspapers under his bed,
even my first painting.

As we signed the papers, Marco and I took each other's hand and tears of joy came down our cheeks.

Our son Ambrose was growing up. He was going to Manhattan to school. I could not supervise him any longer. I spoke with him often and gave him good advice. I am thankful to our Lord that he took the advice we gave him and we never had any problems with him.

Marco was working in Brooklyn for a company called Alliance that made all kinds of Architectural woodwork including furniture. One day he came home.

"Guess what I am working on today," he joked with us. We begged him to tell us.

"I am making a display case that is going to Washington, DC. They are going to put the rocks that came from the moon in the two pieces I am making to display the moon rocks."

Sonia, left, at her first U.S. job in Brooklyn

After he had finished the display case and it had been sent to Washington, we went to the Smithsonian Space Museum and we saw the cases that Marco had made. I was so proud of Marco and I was also very proud to be an American. When we had been in the U.S. long enough, we applied and became naturalized American Citizens.

As for my work, a few people told me that I should be working in Manhattan. My answer was always about my need to supervise my son but those days were over.

One day as I was thinking, I said to myself, if a hundred thousand people get to Manhattan to work, why shouldn't I go? I called a friend that was working with me. She was also Italian and her name was Lina Ianno. I told her that she had talked about going to work in Manhattan. I told her that if she would go, I would come to. She told me she already had an address. She said she would go and see what there was and then let me know.

Two days later she called me. She asked me if I still wanted to come to see what work there was. I told her yes.

We went together to this place that made expensive sweaters. The company however wanted to open a new product line of dresses and shoes under the name SEMPLICE.

Lina and I were doing very well in our jobs. The company executives liked our work very much. We asked more questions and we found out they had no union. We both talked things over and we agreed we had to find another job before the time expired and we would lose our union book.

Going home on the subway one day, Lina and I met a lady that lived on our block. She spoke to us, saying that she had seen us in the neighborhood.

"I know you," she said, "you work on dresses. I do that too but because the boss isn't making money, the place where I work is closing. The place made low cost dresses and the boss has been given an offer to be the manager of a new department that the Lesley Fay Company just bought. The department is called Kasper and they are going to make samples to send for productions. He needs sample makers."

The lady gave me the name and phone number of the manager. His name was Arthur Smilowitz. My friend Lina called him the next day and he said to come to his location on 34th and Broadway. The next day we went to see him and he gave me a suit, jacket, skirt and a blouse. When he saw our work, he said, "I have nothing to say. You work very well. The next thing he said to us was, that yesterday was his lucky day. It was not easy to find workers like Lina and me. After Kasper, the company also bought Nolan Millers Dynasty Collection, the designer for the television show.

I have a lot for which to thank our Lord. I retired after many years. Marco was already retired. When I retired, we talked about moving out of Brooklyn.

Florida and Maryland
2011

BY that time our son Ambrose was married and had three children: Stephen, Jon-Michael and Allison. After our retirement, Ambrose was transferred to Florida. They bought a house in Sunrise Florida.

It wasn't too long before Marco and I decided we should move to Florida also. We sold our house in Brooklyn and we bought a home in Davie, Florida.

Ambrose was not done traveling as it turned out. He ended up being transferred to Maryland. We told him we were not moving from Florida until it was time for us to move home to the Lord.

But, after 20 years in Florida, we realized we were getting old and decided to look at homes for the elderly. We searched and found one that we liked and again, we put our house on the market. It didn't sell right away.

One night, when we were in bed sleeping, I was awakened suddenly as if someone had shaken me. When I opened my eyes, I looked around. As if my mind made our decision about where to move. I suddenly realized we had to move to be near our son.

"Marco," I said, as I woke him up," what are we doing? Here we are thinking of going to a home for seniors in Tamarac. What about Ambrose? When we get older and sick, he will just have to go back and forth from Maryland? We are making a big mistake. We have to sacrifice Florida and think about our son!"

"You are right," Marco said. "We did not think things through. We'll call Ambrose in the morning to hear what he thinks about this."

That same morning we called Ambrose and told him what we had discussed.

"Mom, Dad," Ambrose began, "I did not want to say anything because you had to make the decision but I am very happy that you have changed your mind about where you want to be. You can come to Maryland and we will visit several places and see which one you might like."

We told him to start to look for places not too far from where he lived. Soon he found one that he liked and he told us to come up and see it.

The place he found was in Leonardtown, a place called Cedar Lane.

We made our reservation and we went to Maryland. We saw a couple of senior homes but we went back to the first one that Ambrose had found. We told the managers that when we sold our home in Florida, we would get in touch with them.

In August 2011, we sold our home and once more, we moved. We told each other that we hoped this was the last move before the Lord called us home.

Many years have passed since Marco and I were married. It has been exactly 66 years since we exchanged our vows. We are still together and in love. When someone asked me how we did it, I tell them that marriage is about give and take. If you want your marriage to work, you have to remember that love is always stronger than bickering.

This is the story of Sonia Di Tommaso Cucinotta, a teenager growing up during the battles of the occupation of Anzio during World War II. I thank our Lord for having saved us many times from death, for being with us during the struggle, hunger, despair that we passed through alive

This page is dedicated to Dr. Fillipo and Miggs Ferrigni. They came to visit us one year in Florida, and while reminiscing about the old days, they encouraged us to write the story down as a possible book. I responded, at my age and after so many years? They answered, why not; you lived it and alive today! With Miggs's patience, my story is done.

I thank you Miggs and Fillipo, for your patience and support throughout this effort.

Sonia Di Tommaso Cucinotta

Thank You

I want to thank you from the bottom of my heart, our daughter-in-law Darlene, for helping us move to Maryland, where we live today.

Marco and I got very sick and with Darlene's help and knowledge of medicine, being a nurse, she saved our lives. If it wasn't for her, the last pages of this book might not have been written.

Thank you, again, and God bless you, dear Darlene.

To our dear son, Ambrose, for being there for us along the path of our lives and to have become an honest man. For us, it was something that we always taught him and are proud of. For all the help he has given us in putting the papers and photos together to make it look like a book.

To Amy Bush, from the Holocaust Museum, in Washington, D.C., for helping me locate a particular event that was hard to find. Also, Celia Rabinowitz, at Saint Mary's College, in Maryland, for helping me find the books I needed to complete my story.

To Don Luigi Bozoni from the Salesian Monastery on the Appia Antica in Rome and referred me to Don Francesco Motto, a historian in Rome. In his reference that relates to the story of the Fosse Ardeatine, he mentions the Di Tommaso family, as coming from Pomezia as refugees to the Salesian Monastery.

A very special thank you to my nephew, Vincenzo Blancodini, and his staff of La Fenice Grafica, in Pomezia, Italy, for producing the first pre-publication issues of this book.

For the Jewish Boys

I hope that they are still alive. I was happy to have known them and the fond memories of their friendship. If by some chance they get to read this book, please contact the publisher.

Sonia Di Tommaso

People that Have Touched Our Lives

FRANCE

Norma Lacchio
Harvy Delzet
Alphonse and Marie Perocheau
Giuseppe and Marie Zamma and Family

ITALY

Abruzzo

Blancodini Family
Caterina Libonati and Family

Sicily

Salvatore and Maria Anditore and Family
Ambrogio Cucinotta, nephew
Vincenza Cucinotta, niece
Enza Cucinotta, sister-in-law
Salvatore La Rosa and Family, very close friends
Salvatore Magali and Family

Pomezia

Dino Blancodini, Nephew Enzo and Anca Blancodini Enrico
    and Gabriella Blancodini Alessandro Blancodini
Martina Blancodini
Dario Blancodini, 2nd Nephew
Cinzia Blancodini Comin Family Loreto Di Tommaso

Andrea and Carmela Mezzina
Nardi Family
Elia Trentini

Alba Caccavello and Family

Rome

Dr. Italo Casale and Family
Giacomo Giaime

Sezze Romano

Lidano and Angelina Ciarlo and Family

USA

Brooklyn

John and Ann Adesso and Family Louie and Pat Adorno and Family Mike and Lidia Anciotta
Vinicio and Lisa Bianchi Antonio Conte and Family Culotta Family
Connie D'Angelo and Family Victoria and Frank Joseph Galante Ralph and Victoria Hillman Eduardo Impeiri and Family
Lina Inno and Family
Anthony and Seena Intersimone and Family
Steve and Mimi Lamia
Carmina Lousardi and Family
Phil and Sadie Mazza and Family
Matrisciani Family
Filomena Romano and Family
Mike and Sophie Sacco and Family
Maria Torro and Family

Antoinette and Patricia Trocino

Florida

Mike and Pat Bolinger
Mary Bober
Ralph and Rita Chiofalo
John and Amelia De Vito
Carol Howe
Tony Iovino and Adriana
Monroe and Martin Kiar
Catherine Loupari
Dave Mac Daniel and Family
Nancy Mechaber
Raffaele Nicosia
Emilio Petrov and Family
Tom and Linda Podesta
Rev. Edmond Prendergast
Santa Riegler
Russel and Julie Sweeten
Jean Salerno
Joseph Sardo
Ken Saunders and Family
Michael and Louisa Spatafino
Brenda and Tom Stone and Family
William and Mary Tetro
Flino and Antonoinette Tizzani

Maryland

Jo and Marian Mondo
Kern and Sharron Barrow and Family
Cera Baumbach
Reverend David Beaubien
Bobby Briggs and Carol
Mike and Amy Gibson and Family
Victoria Irvin

Verna Keesee
Kelly and Lori Major
Emma Morris
Scott and Christina Martin and Family
Nicholas Midgett
Janice Pruitt
Christine Senese
Beverly Stickles

www.ingramcontent.com/pod-product-compliance
Lightning Source LLC
LaVergne TN
LVHW051647080426
835511LV00016B/2533